FACE PAINTING
FOR KIDS

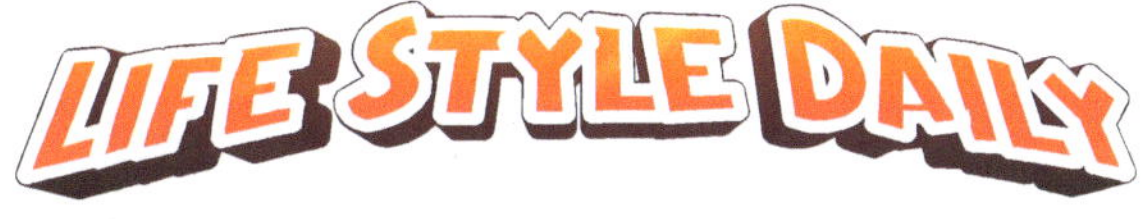

Face Painting Instructions for Children – Step by Step

1. Preparation

Find the right place: Make sure you have a well–lit workspace. Lay out all the tools and paints on a clean surface.

Wash your hands: Always wash your hands before starting face painting.

Check the child's skin: Ensure the child's skin is clean and dry. You can use mild soap and water, then pat the face dry with a towel.

2. Preparing Tools and Paints

Choose the paints: Use non–toxic, hypoallergenic, water–based face paints.

Brushes and sponges: Prepare various brush sizes (thin for details, medium for outlines, thick for filling) and small sponges for applying paint to larger areas.

Water and bowl: Have a bowl of clean water to dampen brushes and sponges and to clean them between colors.

Tissues and paper towels: Have tissues to wipe off excess paint from brushes and sponges and to keep things tidy.

3. Applying the Base

Choose a base color: Apply the base paint using a sponge. Lightly dampen the sponge in water, dip it in paint, and apply to the child's face to create a smooth, even layer.

Allow to dry: Let the base paint dry for a few minutes before proceeding to the next step.

4. Adding Outlines and Design

Drawing outlines: Use a thin brush to outline the design. The outlines should be delicate but clear. You can use black paint for sharp lines.

Adding details: Start adding details such as eyes, noses, stripes, or dots. Use thin brushes for precise lines.

5. Filling in Colors

Filling inside the outlines: Use medium and large brushes to fill in colors inside the outlines. You can also use a sponge for larger areas.

Shading and blending: To achieve a shading effect, use a sponge to gently blend the paints. You can apply a lighter color in the center and a darker one on the edges to create depth.

6. Finishing and Extras

Special effects: Add glitter if you want the design to be more sparkly. Make sure the glitter is safe to use on skin.

Checking the design: Ensure all lines are clear and the colors are well filled in. You can fix any imperfections with a thin brush.

7. Cleaning and Safety

Washing tools: After finishing the painting, thoroughly wash brushes and sponges with warm, soapy water. Let them air dry.

Safety: Always test the paints on a small patch of skin to ensure the child is not allergic. Avoid painting too close to the child's eyes and mouth.

Removing the paint: Water-based paints easily wash off with warm water and mild soap. Use a soft cloth or cotton pad to gently remove the paint from the face.

Face Painting Instructions: Parrot Theme – Step by Step

Tools and Materials:

Face paints: yellow, blue, orange, black

Brushes: thin, medium, and large

Sponge

Bowl of water

Tissues and paper towels

Mirror

Step 1: Prepare the Skin

Wash and dry the child's face.

Step 2: Apply the Yellow Base

Use a sponge to apply yellow paint to the center of the face, particularly on the forehead, nose, and middle of the cheeks. Let it dry.

Step 3: Add Blue Accents

Use a medium brush to add blue accents around the eyes and on the outer parts of the cheeks. Blend the colors smoothly. Let it dry.

Step 4: Add Orange Accents

Use a medium brush to add orange accents on the lower cheeks and around the mouth. Ensure the colors blend seamlessly. Let it dry.

Step 5: Draw Black Details

Use a thin brush and black paint to draw the pattern's outlines, such as lines around the eyes and details on the forehead. Add fine lines to create a feather effect. You can also add black dots on the cheeks.

Step 6: Add Additional Details

Use a thin brush to add more color accents on the face, creating a more realistic parrot look. You can also add white dots to make the design more dynamic.

Step 7: Finishing Touches

Ensure all lines are clear and the colors are well filled in. Show the child the final design in a mirror.

Step 8: Clean Up

Wash brushes and sponges with warm, soapy water. Test paints on a small skin area before painting.

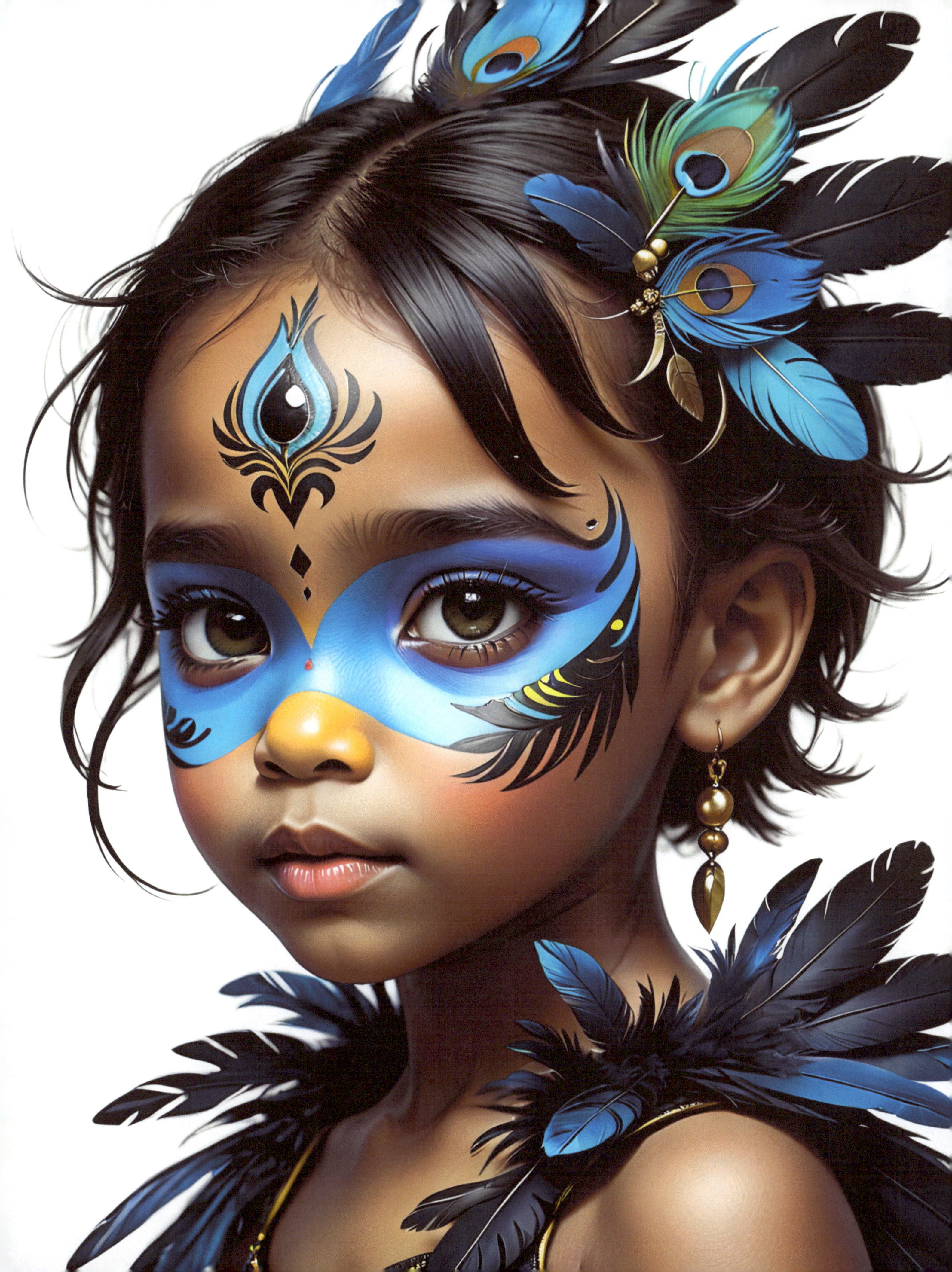

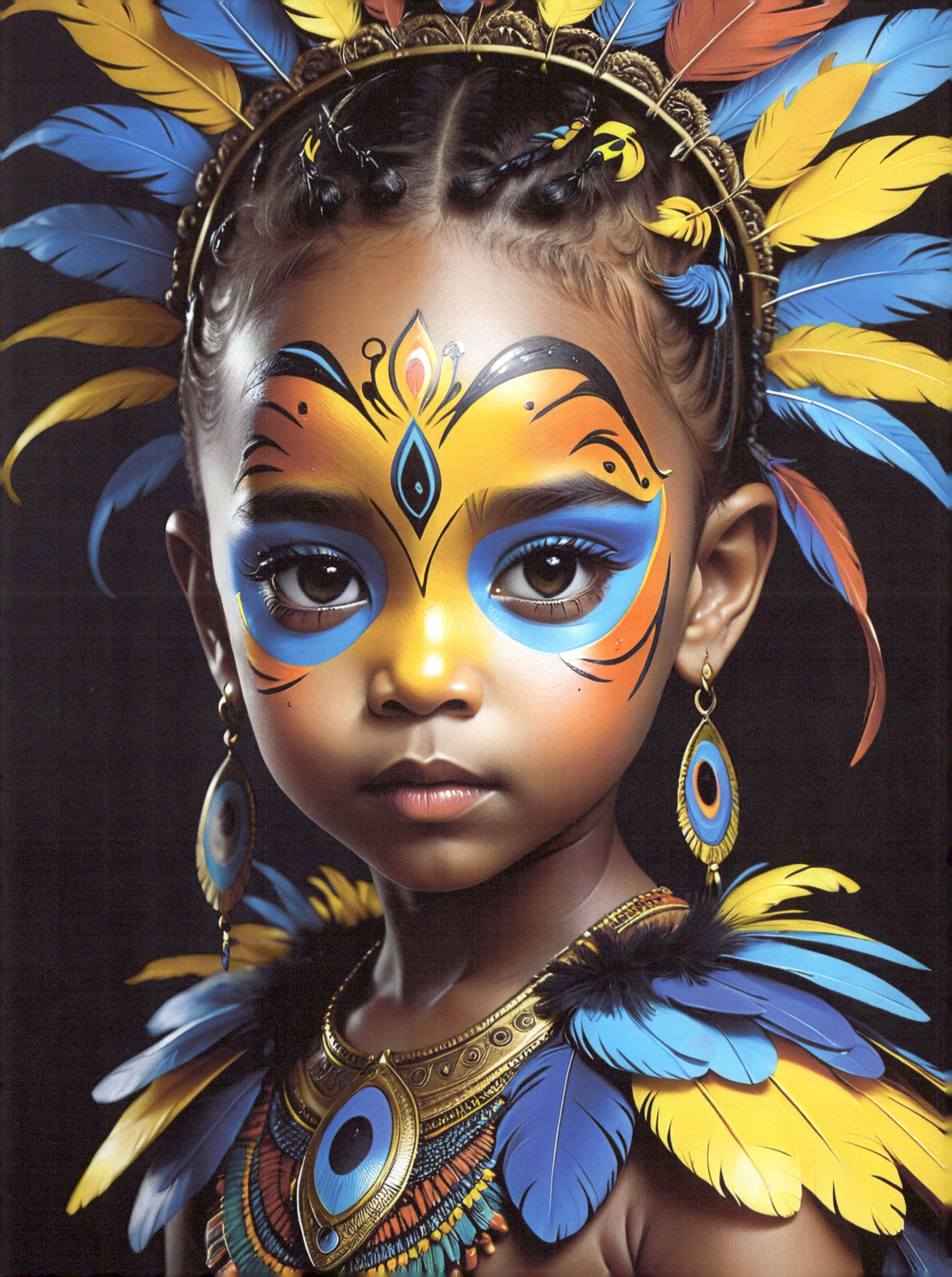

Face Painting Instructions: Koala Theme – Step by Step

Tools and Materials:

Face paints: gray, white, black

Brushes: thin and medium

Sponge

Bowl of water

Tissues and paper towels

Mirror

Step 1: Prepare the Skin

Wash and dry the child's face.

Step 2: Apply the Gray Base

Use a sponge to apply gray paint on the cheeks and forehead, creating the main structure of the koala pattern. Let it dry.

Step 3: Add White Accents

Use a medium brush and white paint to add white accents in the center of the forehead, around the eyes, and on the cheeks. Create shapes resembling the koala's fur. Let it dry.

Step 4: Draw Black Details

Use a thin brush and black paint to draw the nose shape on the tip of the child's nose.

Add black outlines around the white accents to give them definition.

Draw small black dots on the cheeks for extra detail.

Step 5: Add Details on Forehead and Cheeks

Use a thin brush to add additional white and black accents on the forehead and cheeks, creating a more realistic koala look.

Step 6: Finishing Touches

Ensure all lines are clear and the colors are well filled in. Show the child the final design in a mirror.

Step 7: Clean Up

Wash brushes and sponges with warm, soapy water. Test paints on a small skin area before painting.

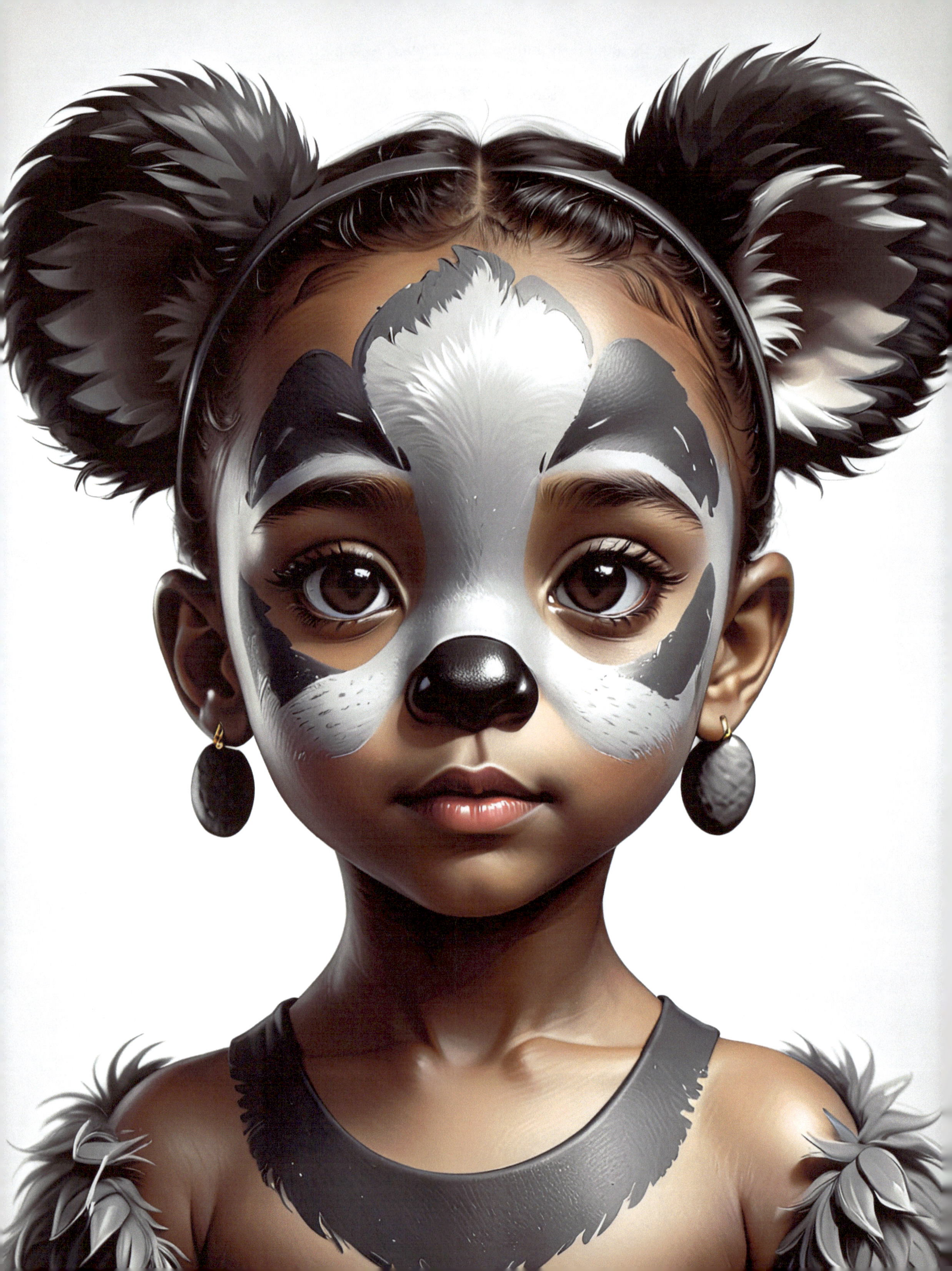

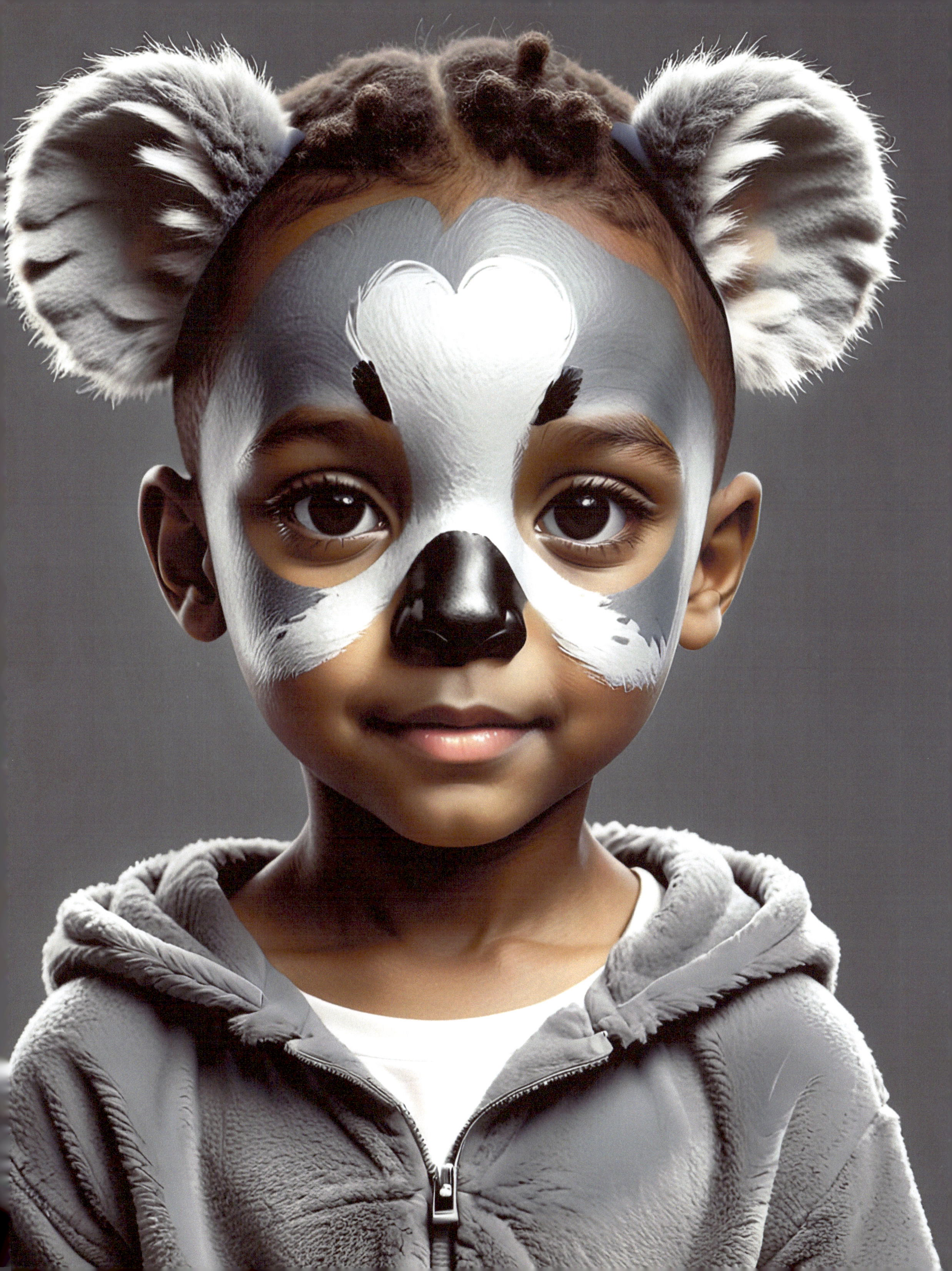

Face Painting Instructions: Chameleon Theme – Step by Step

Tools and Materials:

Face paints: blue, green, orange, black, yellow

Brushes: thin, medium, and large

Sponge

Bowl of water

Tissues and paper towels

Mirror

Step 1: Prepare the Skin

Wash and dry the child's face.

Step 2: Apply the Blue Base

Use a sponge to apply blue paint to the upper part of the face, especially on the forehead and around the eyes. Let it dry.

Step 3: Add Green Accents

Use a medium brush to add green accents to the middle of the face, particularly on the cheeks and nose. Blend the colors smoothly. Let it dry.

Step 4: Add Orange and Yellow Accents

Use a medium brush to add orange accents to the lower cheeks and around the mouth. Add yellow accents in selected areas to highlight details. Ensure the colors blend seamlessly. Let it dry.

Step 5: Draw Black Details

Use a thin brush and black paint to draw the pattern's outlines, such as lines around the eyes, on the forehead, and nose. Add fine lines and dots to create a scale effect. You can also add black dots on the cheeks.

Step 6: Add Additional Details

Use a thin brush to add more color accents on the face, creating a more realistic chameleon look. You can also add white dots to make the design more dynamic.

Step 7: Finishing Touches

Ensure all lines are clear and the colors are well filled in. Show the child the final design in a mirror.

Step 8: Clean Up

Wash brushes and sponges with warm, soapy water. Test paints on a small skin area before painting.

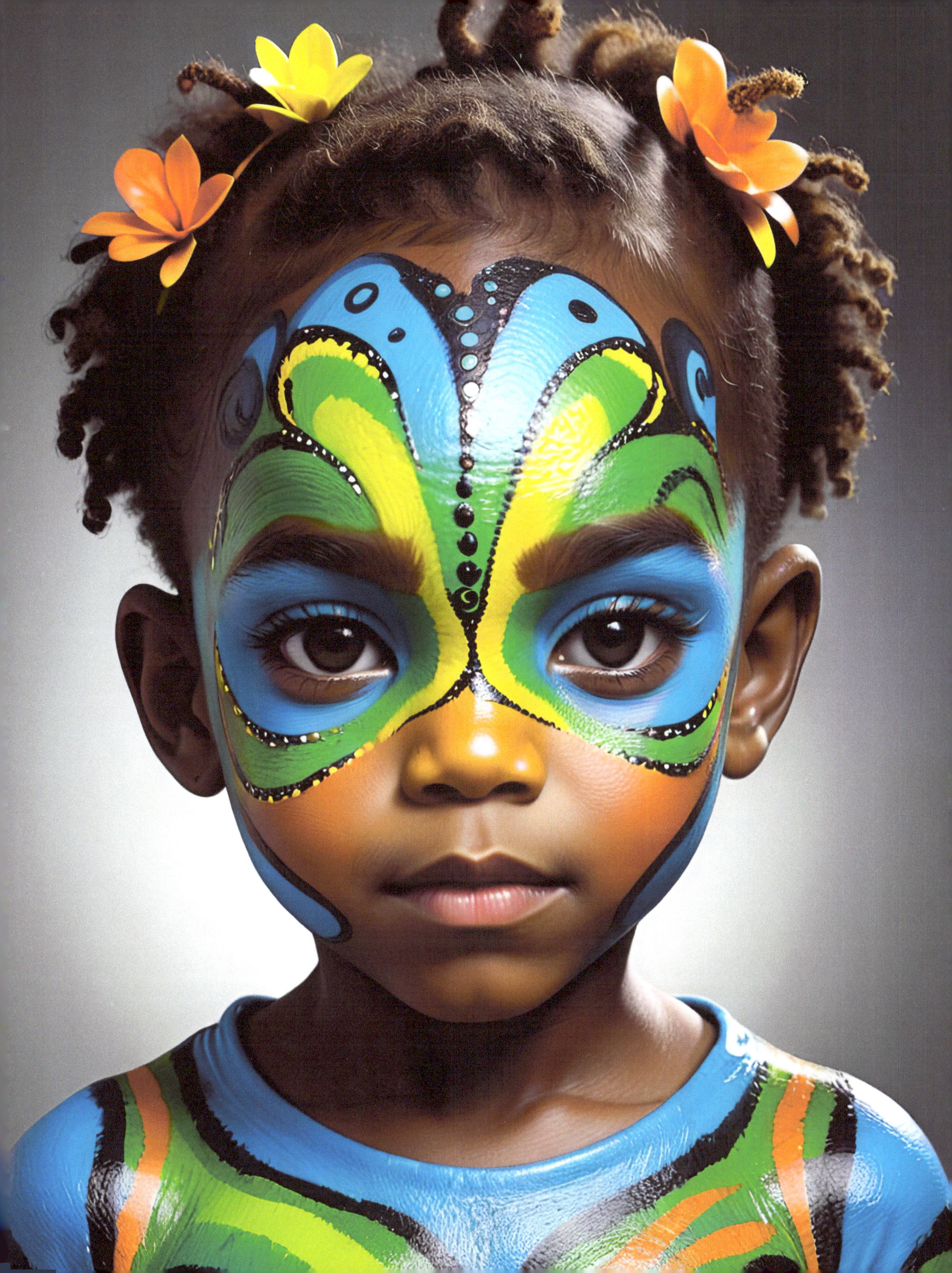

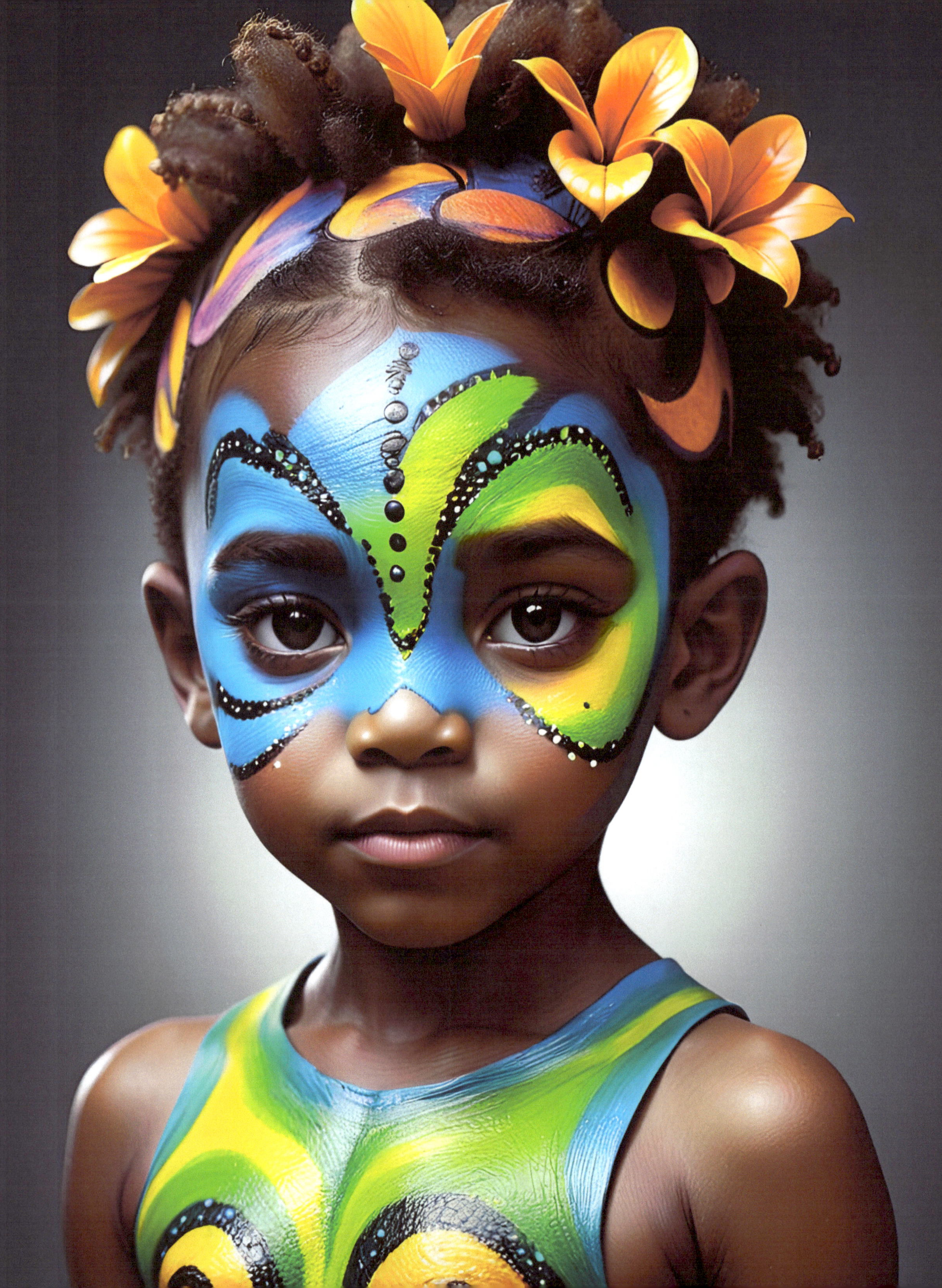

Face Painting Instructions: Cosmic Elf Theme – Step by Step

Tools and Materials:

Face paints: blue, white, black

Brushes: thin, medium, and large

Sponge

Bowl of water

Tissues and paper towels

Mirror

Step 1: Prepare the Skin

Wash and dry the child's face.

Step 2: Apply the Blue Base

Use a sponge to apply blue paint over the entire face, creating a uniform base. Let it dry.

Step 3: Add Darker and Lighter Blue Accents

Use a medium brush to add darker blue accents on the forehead, cheeks, and around the eyes. Then add lighter blue accents to the same areas to create depth and dimension. Let it dry.

Step 4: Draw White Patterns

Use a thin brush and white paint to draw cosmic elf–inspired patterns on the forehead, cheeks, and nose. Use small dots, lines, and spirals to create the effect of bioluminescent markings. Let it dry.

Step 5: Add Black Details

Use a thin brush and black paint to add subtle outlines around the white patterns and eyes to emphasize their shape and give definition. You can also add small black accents on the temples and around the hairline.

Step 6: Add Additional Details

Use a thin brush to add small white and blue dots around the face to complete the pattern. You can also add delicate white lines on the cheeks and forehead to create a luminous effect.

Step 7: Finishing Touches

Ensure all lines are clear and the colors are well filled in. Show the child the final design in a mirror.

Step 8: Clean Up

Wash brushes and sponges with warm, soapy water. Test paints on a small skin area before painting.

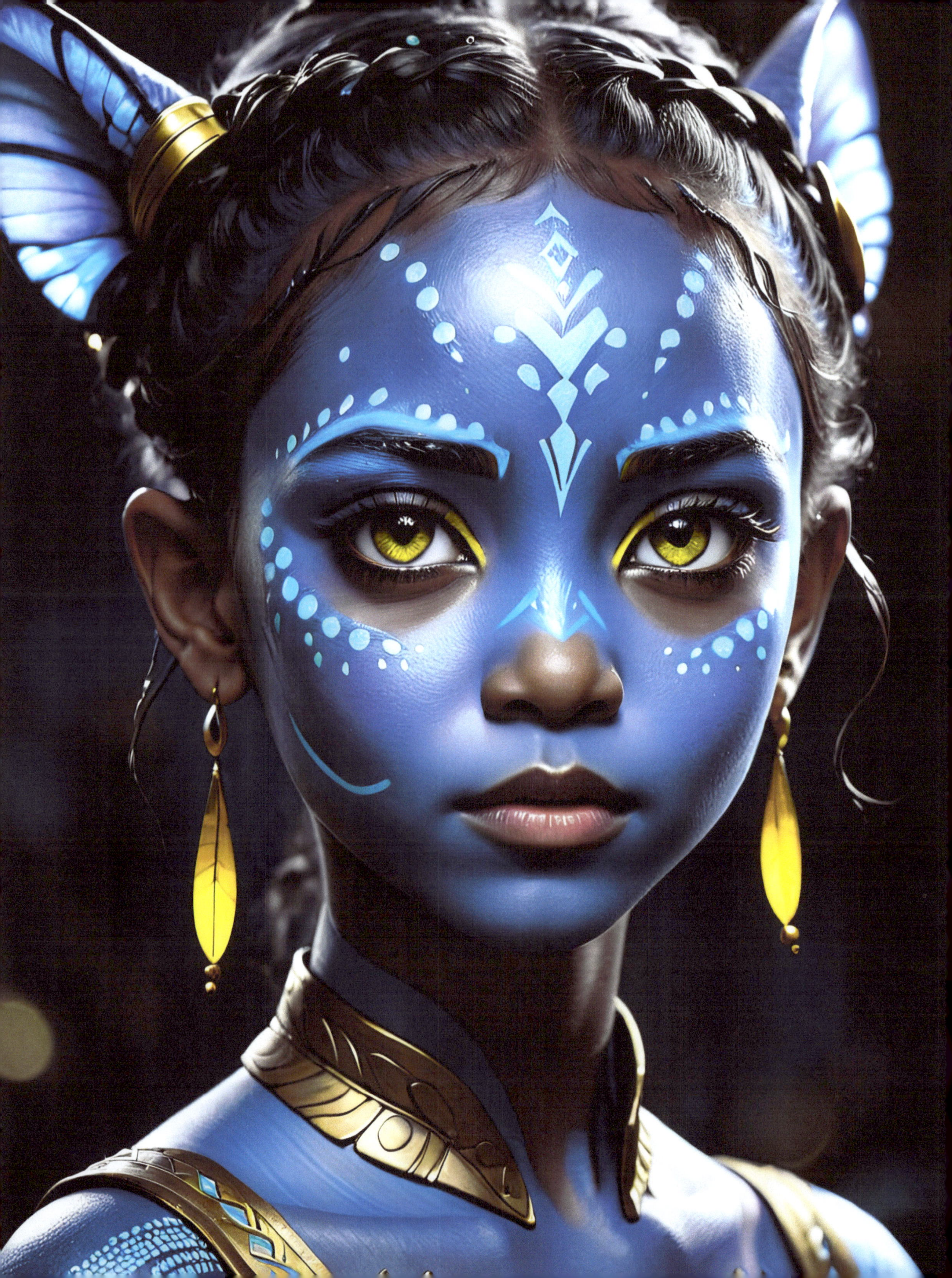

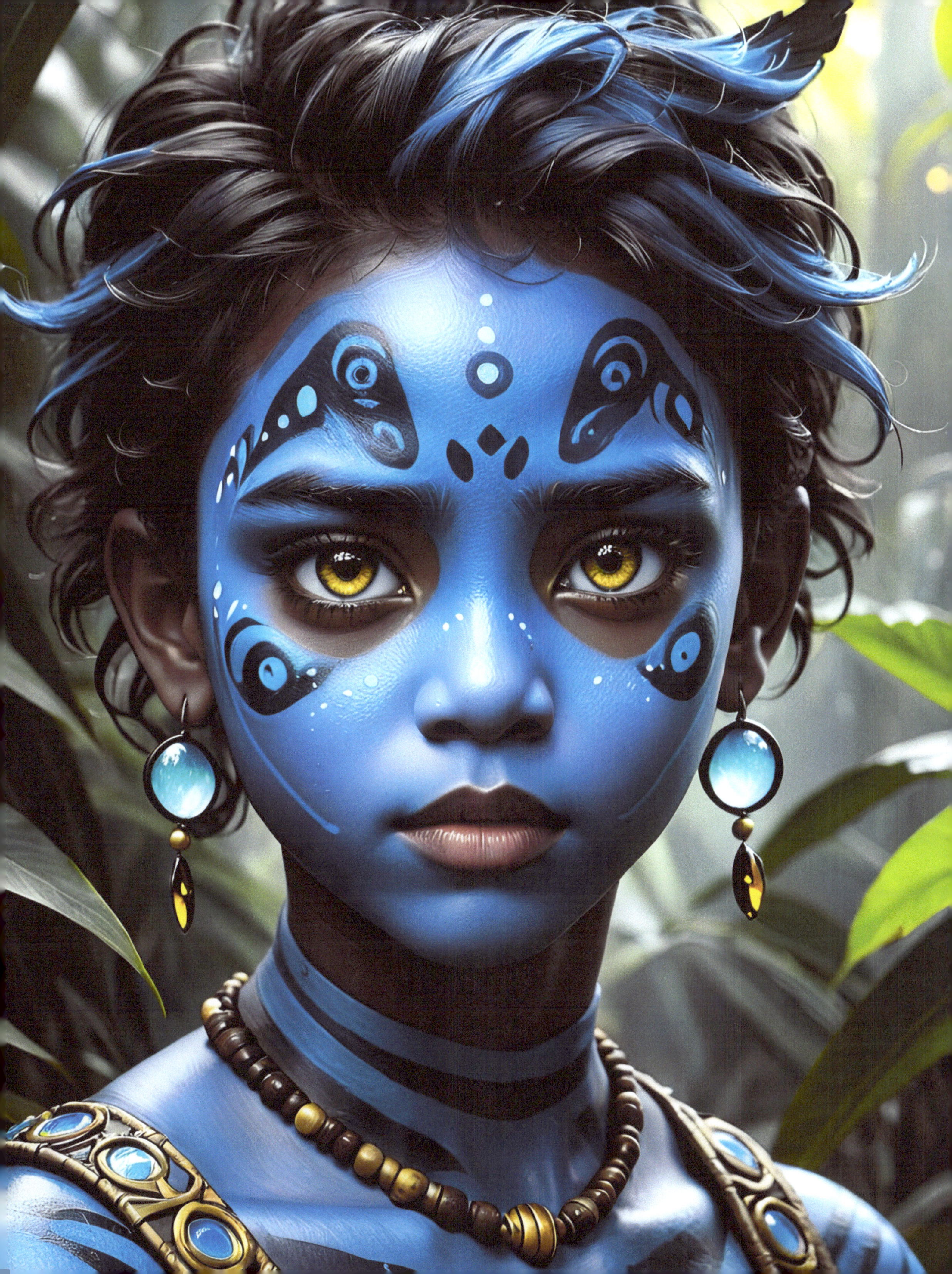

Face Painting Instructions: Black Mouse Costume – Step by Step

Tools and Materials:

Face paints: black

Brushes: thin and medium

Sponge

Bowl of water

Tissues and paper towels

Mirror

Step 1: Prepare the Skin

Wash and dry the child's face.

Step 2: Draw the Black Nose and Ears

Use a thin brush and black paint to draw a small black nose on the tip of the child's nose. Add two oval shapes above the eyebrows to resemble mouse ears.

Step 3: Add Black Stripe and Dots

Use a thin brush to draw a black stripe from the nose upward to the forehead, between the oval ear shapes. Add small black dots on either side of the nose.

Step 4: Finishing Touches

Ensure all lines are clear. Show the child the final design in a mirror.

Step 5: Clean Up

Wash brushes and sponges with warm, soapy water.

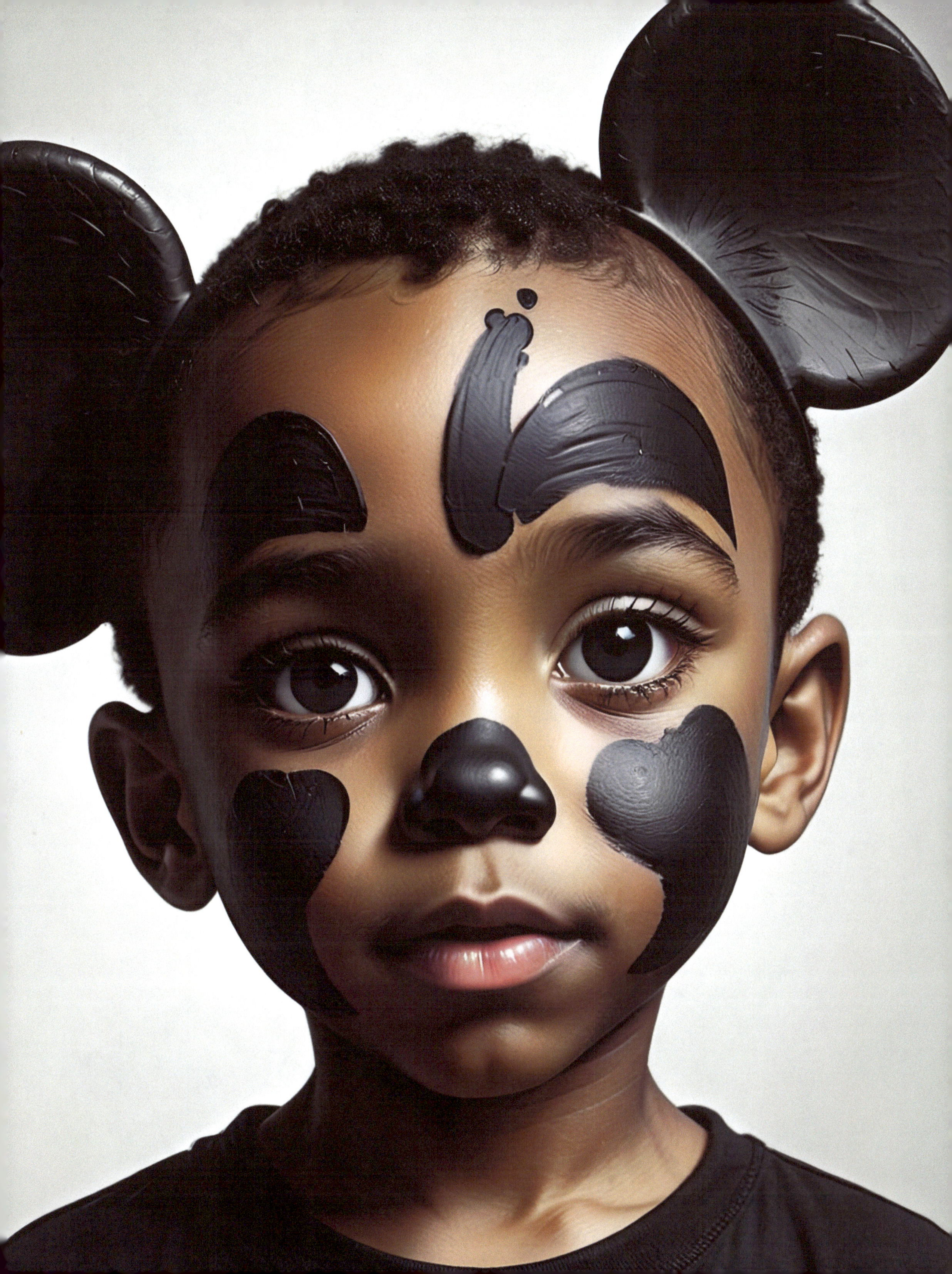

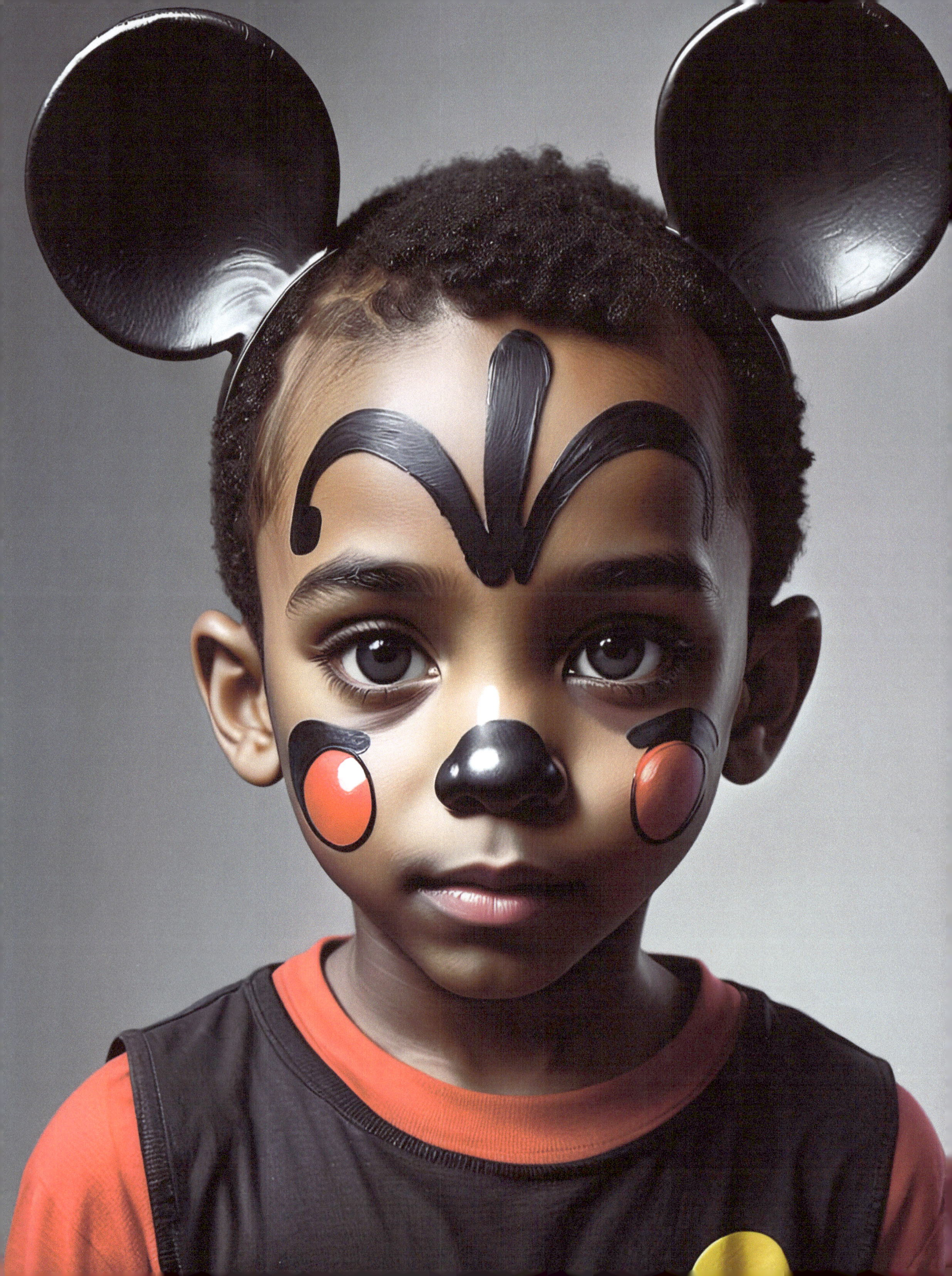

Face Painting Instructions: Red Mouse Costume – Step by Step

Tools and Materials:

Face paints: black, red

Brushes: thin and medium

Sponge

Bowl of water

Tissues and paper towels

Mirror

Step 1: Prepare the Skin

Wash and dry the child's face.

Step 2: Draw the Black Nose

Use a thin brush and black paint to draw a small black nose on the tip of the child's nose. Add small black dots on either side of the nose.

Step 3: Add Red Cheeks

Use a sponge to apply red paint on the cheeks, creating round shapes.

Step 4: Paint the Lips

Use a thin brush to apply red paint on the lips, giving them a vibrant look.

Step 5: Finishing Touches

Ensure all lines are clear and the colors are well filled in. Show the child the final design in a mirror.

Step 6: Clean Up

Wash brushes and sponges with warm, soapy water.

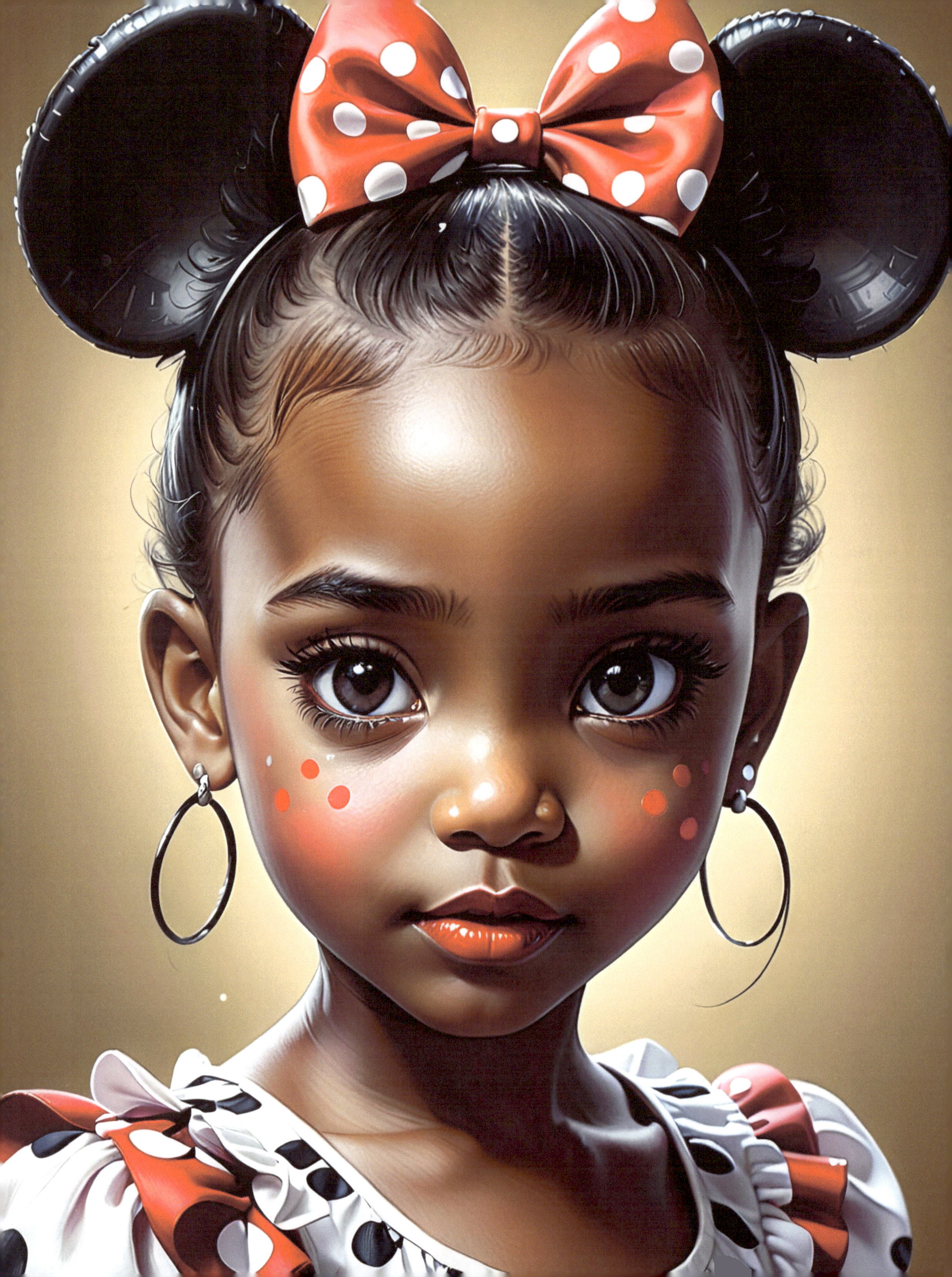

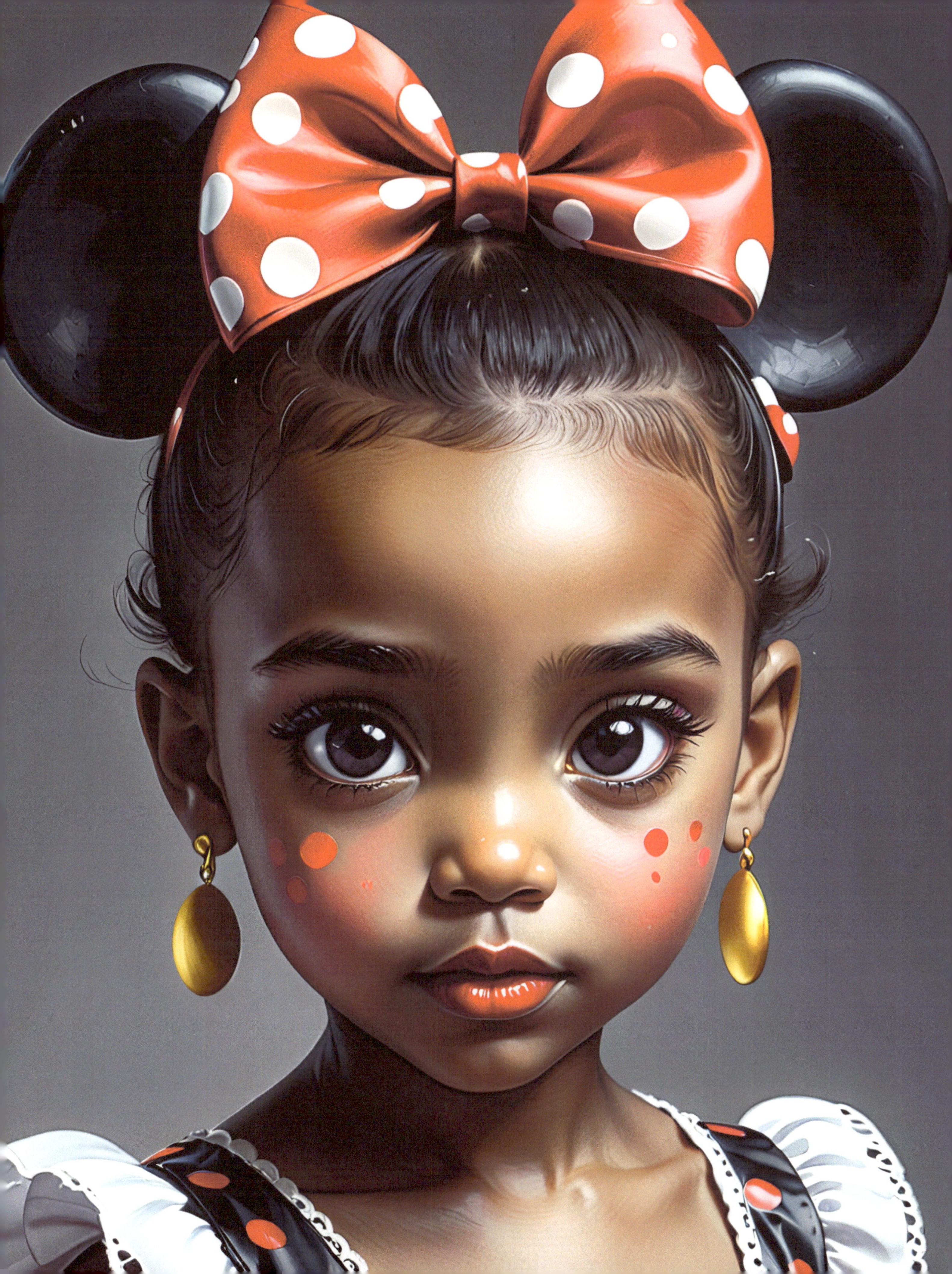

Face Painting Instructions: Spider Mask Theme — Step by Step

Tools and Materials:

Face paints: red, black, white

Brushes: thin, medium, and large

Sponge

Bowl of water

Tissues and paper towels

Mirror

Step 1: Prepare the Skin

Wash and dry the child's face.

Step 2: Apply the Red Base

Use a sponge to apply red paint to the entire face, avoiding the eye and mouth areas. Let it dry.

Step 3: Draw the Spider Web

Use a thin brush and black paint to draw the spider web on the forehead, cheeks, and chin. Start from the center of the face, drawing lines in different directions, then connect them with curved lines to form the web shape.

Step 4: Add Black Details Around the Eyes

Use a thin brush and black paint to outline the area around the eyes, creating the mask shape. Ensure the lines are even and symmetrical.

Step 5: Fill in the Mask Around the Eyes

Fill in the area around the eyes with black paint using a medium brush, leaving space for the white elements.

Step 6: Add White Accents

Use a thin brush and white paint to add white accents to the mask around the eyes. You can also add white dots on the web to give it more depth.

Step 7: Finishing Touches

Ensure all lines are clear and the colors are well filled in. Show the child the final design in a mirror.

Step 8: Clean Up

Wash brushes and sponges with warm, soapy water. Test paints on a small skin area before painting.

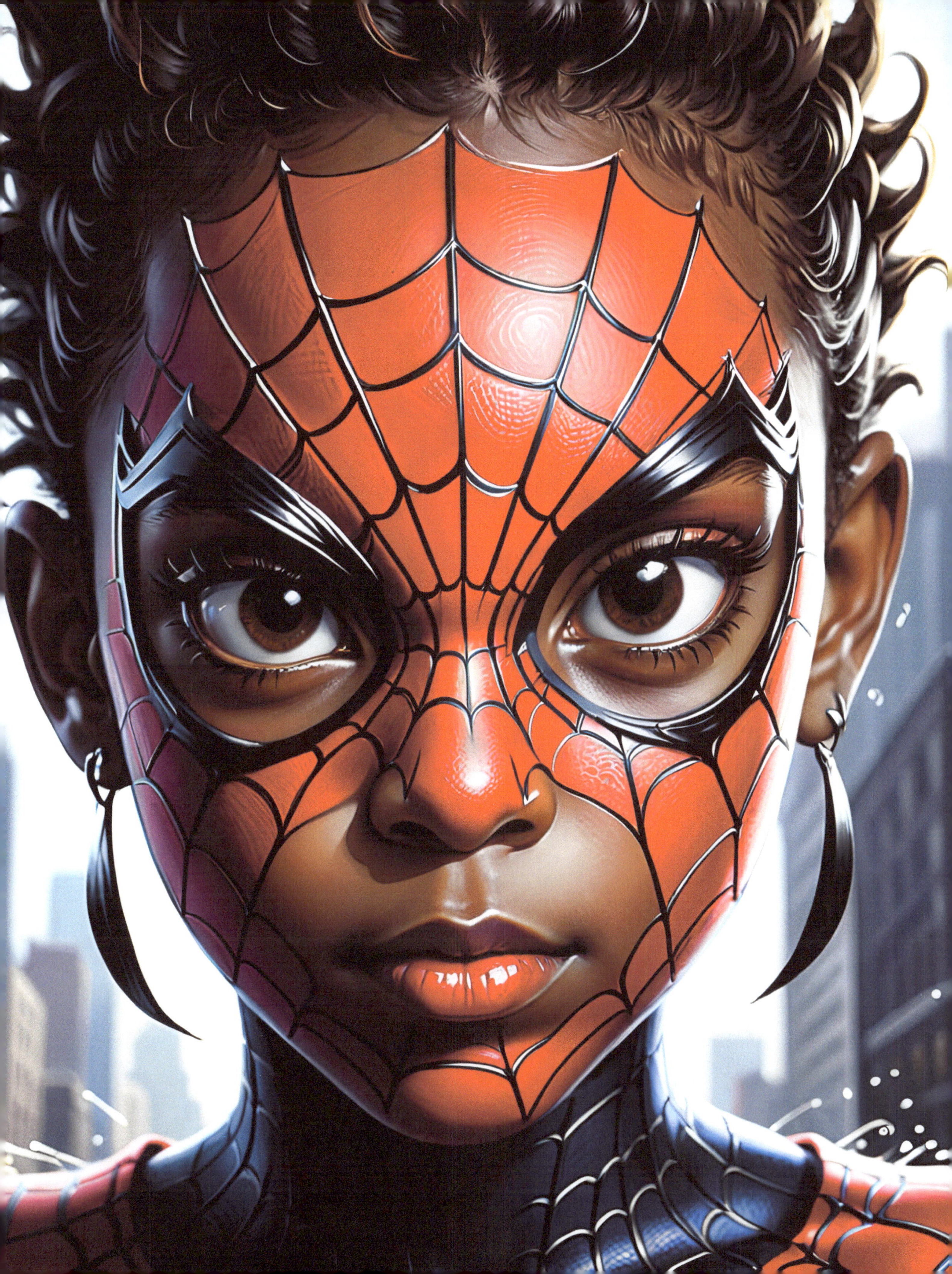

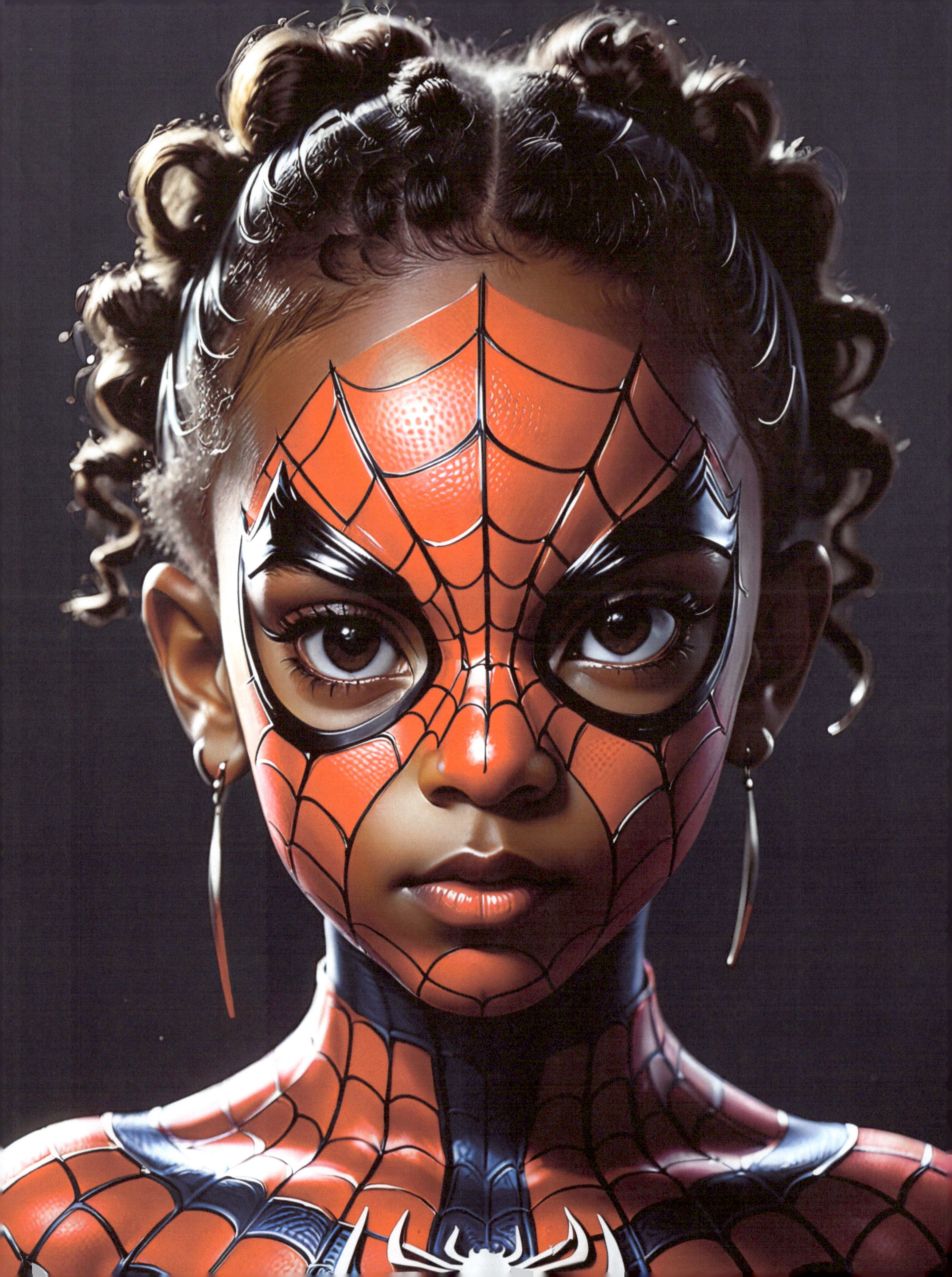

Face Painting Instructions: Electric Creature Theme – Step by Step

Tools and Materials:

Face paints: yellow, red, black

Brushes: thin and medium

Sponge

Bowl of water

Tissues and paper towels

Mirror

Step 1: Prepare the Skin

Wash and dry the child's face.

Step 2: Apply the Yellow Base

Use a sponge to apply yellow paint over the entire face. Let it dry.

Step 3: Draw Red Cheeks

Use a medium brush and red paint to create two large round red cheeks on either side of the face. Let it dry.

Step 4: Add Black Details

Use a thin brush and black paint to draw small lines at the ends of the eyes, creating a distinctive look.

You can also add black lines along the forehead, mimicking the character's hair shape.

Step 5: Finishing Touches

Ensure all lines are clear and the colors are well filled in. Show the child the final design in a mirror.

Step 6: Clean Up

Wash brushes and sponges with warm, soapy water. Test paints on a small skin area before painting.

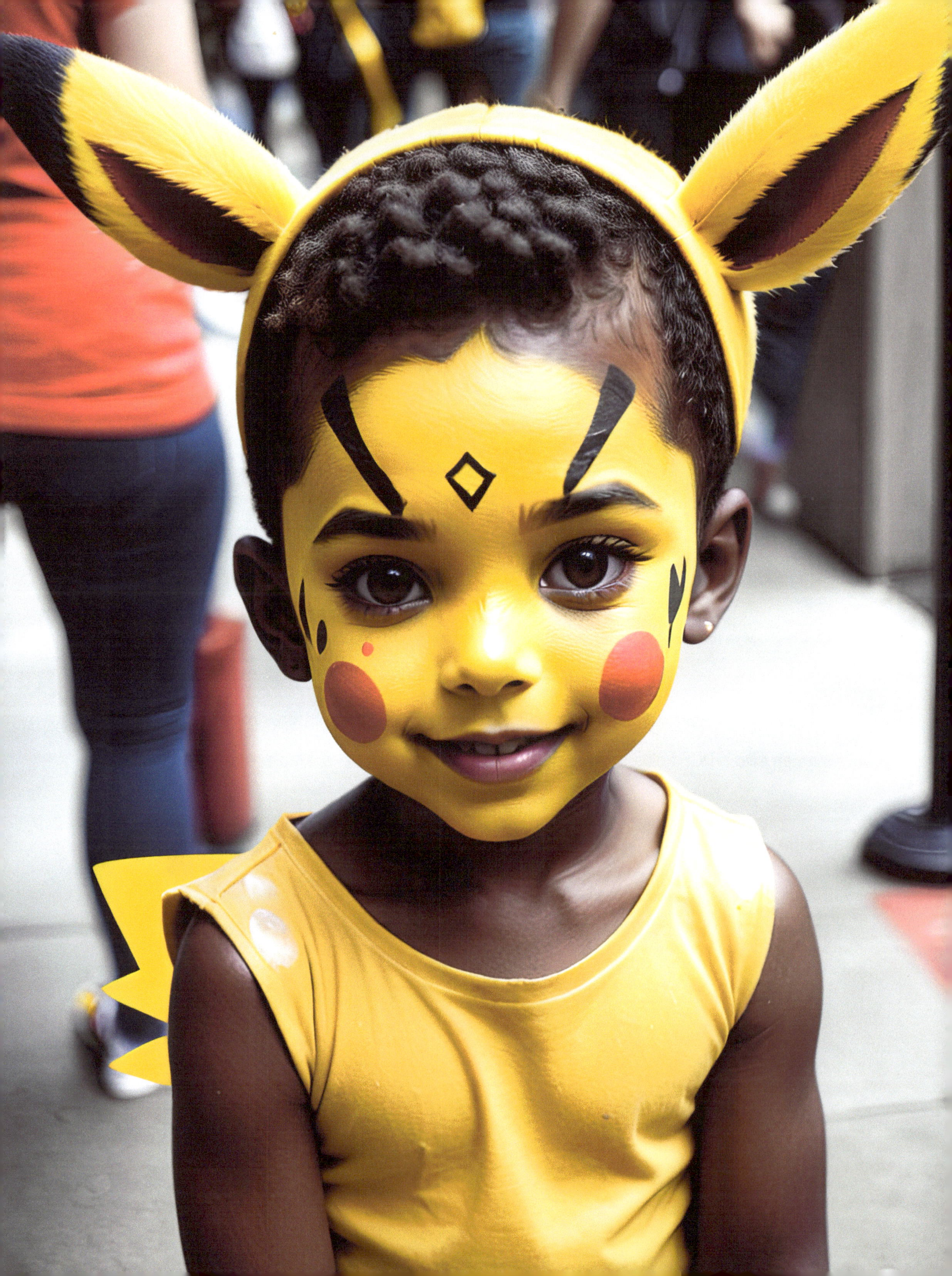

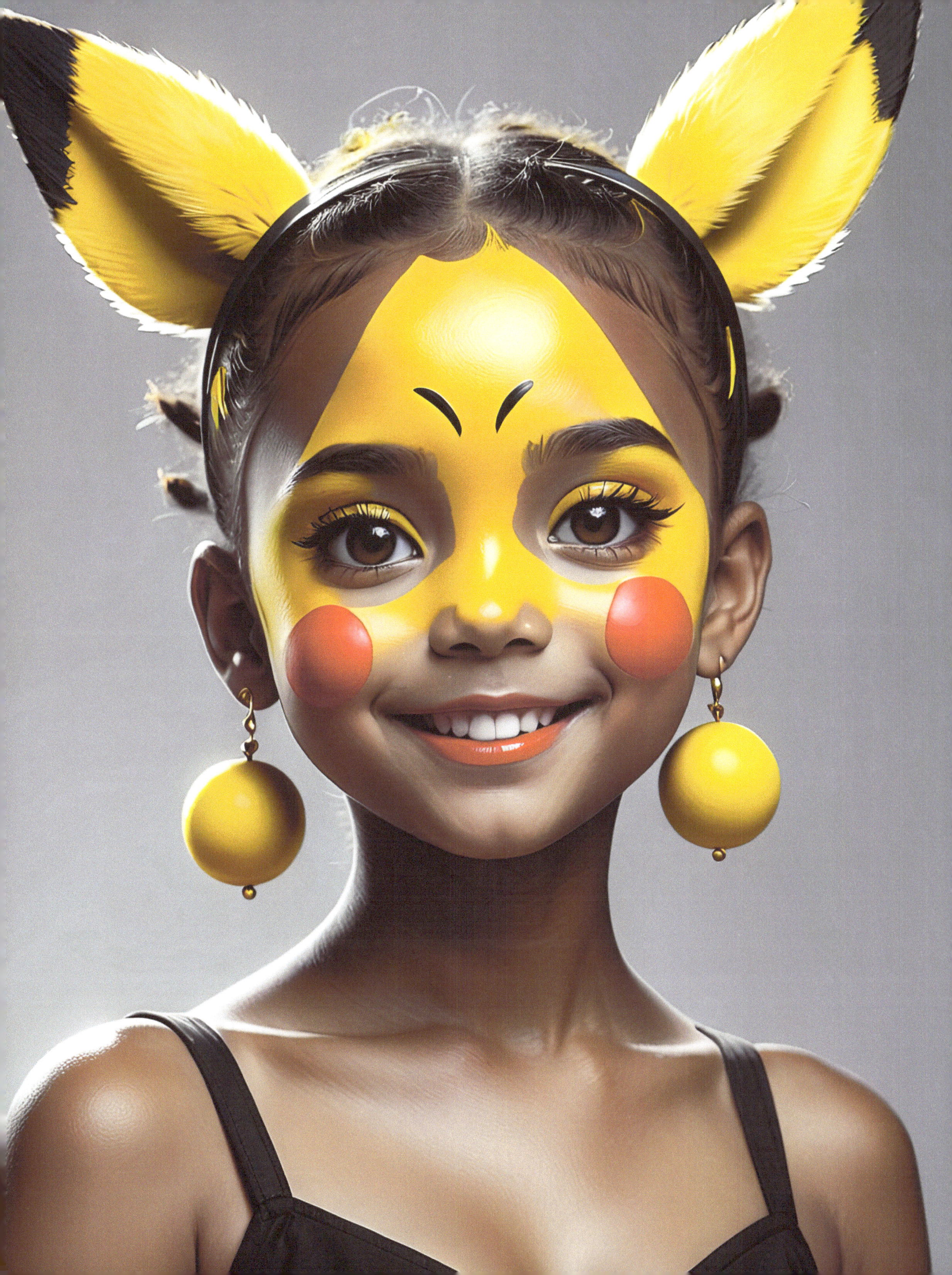

Face Painting Instructions: Young Wizard Theme – Step by Step

Tools and Materials:

Face paints: yellow, black, red

Brushes: thin and medium

Sponge

Bowl of water

Tissues and paper towels

Mirror

Round glasses (if available)

Step 1: Prepare the Skin

Wash and dry the child's face.

Step 2: Draw the Lightning Bolt Scar

Use a thin brush and yellow paint to draw a lightning bolt scar on the child's forehead. Let it dry.

Add shading with black paint to make the scar more pronounced.

Step 3: Draw the Glasses (Optional)

Use a thin brush and black paint to draw round glasses around the child's eyes. Try to make the lines even and clear. Let it dry.

Alternatively: You can simply put round glasses on the child instead of drawing them with paint.

Step 4: Add Face Details

Use a thin brush and black paint to add delicate eyebrow lines and shading around the eyes to give the character a more authentic look.

You can also add a light pink tint on the cheeks to give a healthy appearance.

Step 5: Paint the Robe

Use a medium brush and red paint to create a tie in red and gold colors on the lower part of the face and neck, mimicking the young wizard's attire.

Step 6: Finishing Touches

Ensure all lines are clear and the colors are well filled in. Show the child the final design in a mirror.

Step 7: Clean Up

Wash brushes and sponges with warm, soapy water. Test paints on a small skin area before painting.

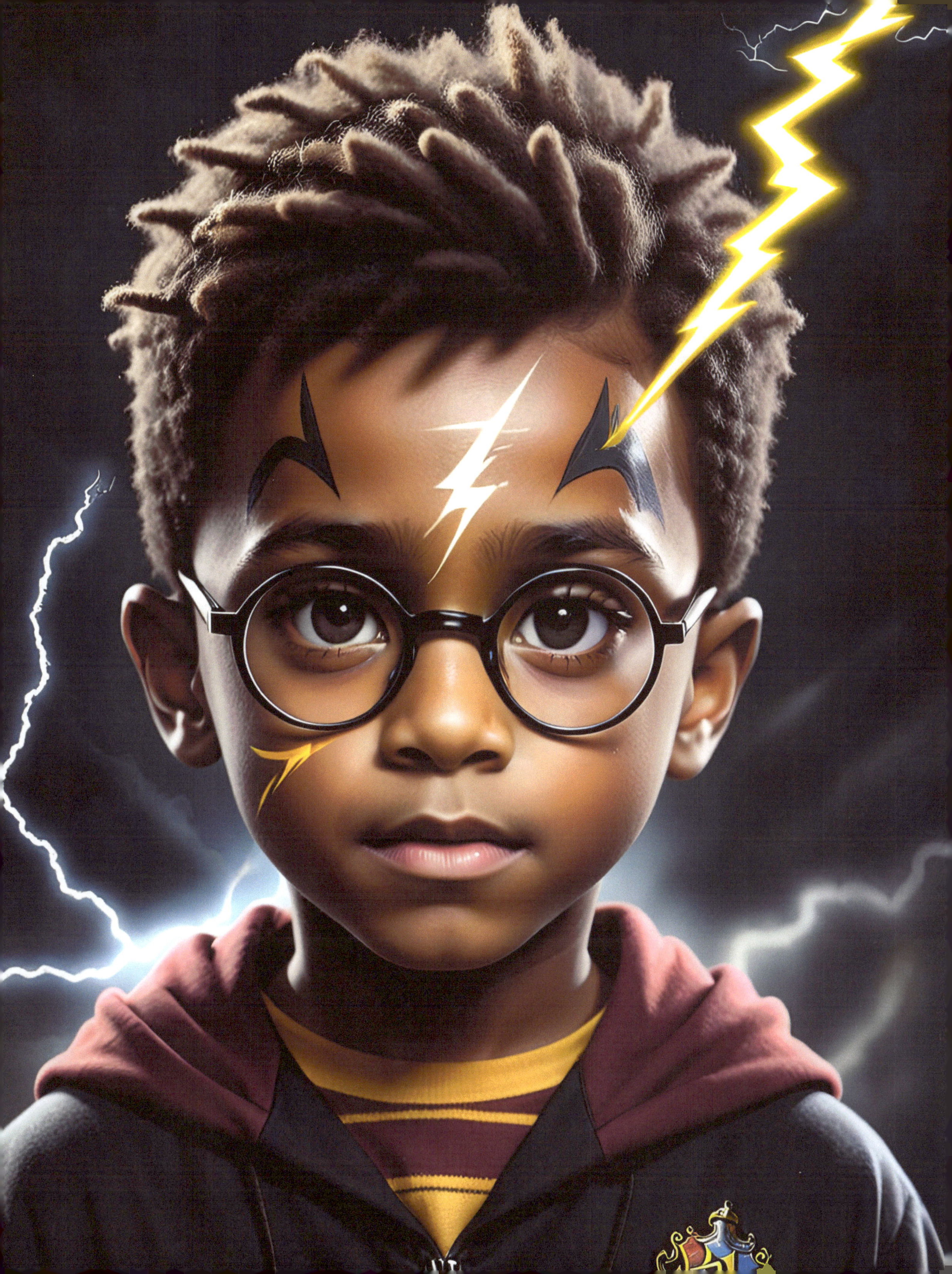

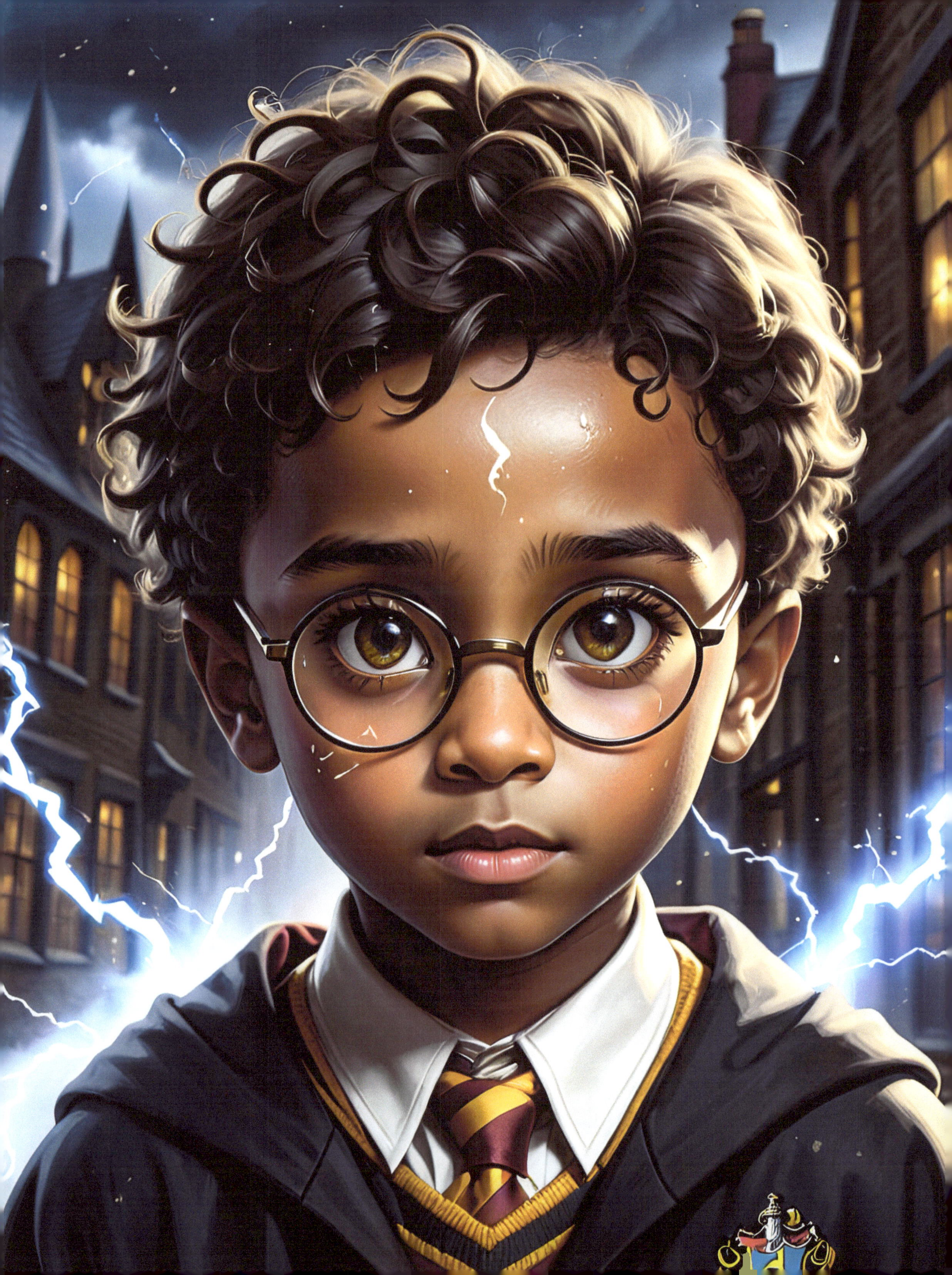

Face Painting Instructions: Yellow Character Theme – Step by Step

Tools and Materials:

Face paints: yellow, black, white

Brushes: thin and medium

Sponge

Bowl of water

Tissues and paper towels

Mirror

Plastic glasses

Step 1: Prepare the Skin

Wash and dry the child's face.

Step 2: Apply the Yellow Base

Use a sponge to apply yellow paint to the entire face, avoiding the eye area. Let it dry.

Step 3: Add Black Details

Use a thin brush and black paint to draw subtle lines around the eyes, serving as a base for the glasses. Add fine lines on the mouth to create a characteristic smile.

Step 4: Add White Accents

Use a thin brush and white paint to add white accents to the smile and possibly subtle shadows around the eyes to highlight the glasses.

Step 5: Put on the Glasses

Place the plastic glasses on the child's nose to complete the character look. Ensure the glasses fit well and are comfortable.

Step 6: Finishing Touches

Ensure all lines are clear and the colors are well filled in. Show the child the final design in a mirror.

Step 7: Clean Up

Wash brushes and sponges with warm, soapy water. Test paints on a small skin area before painting.

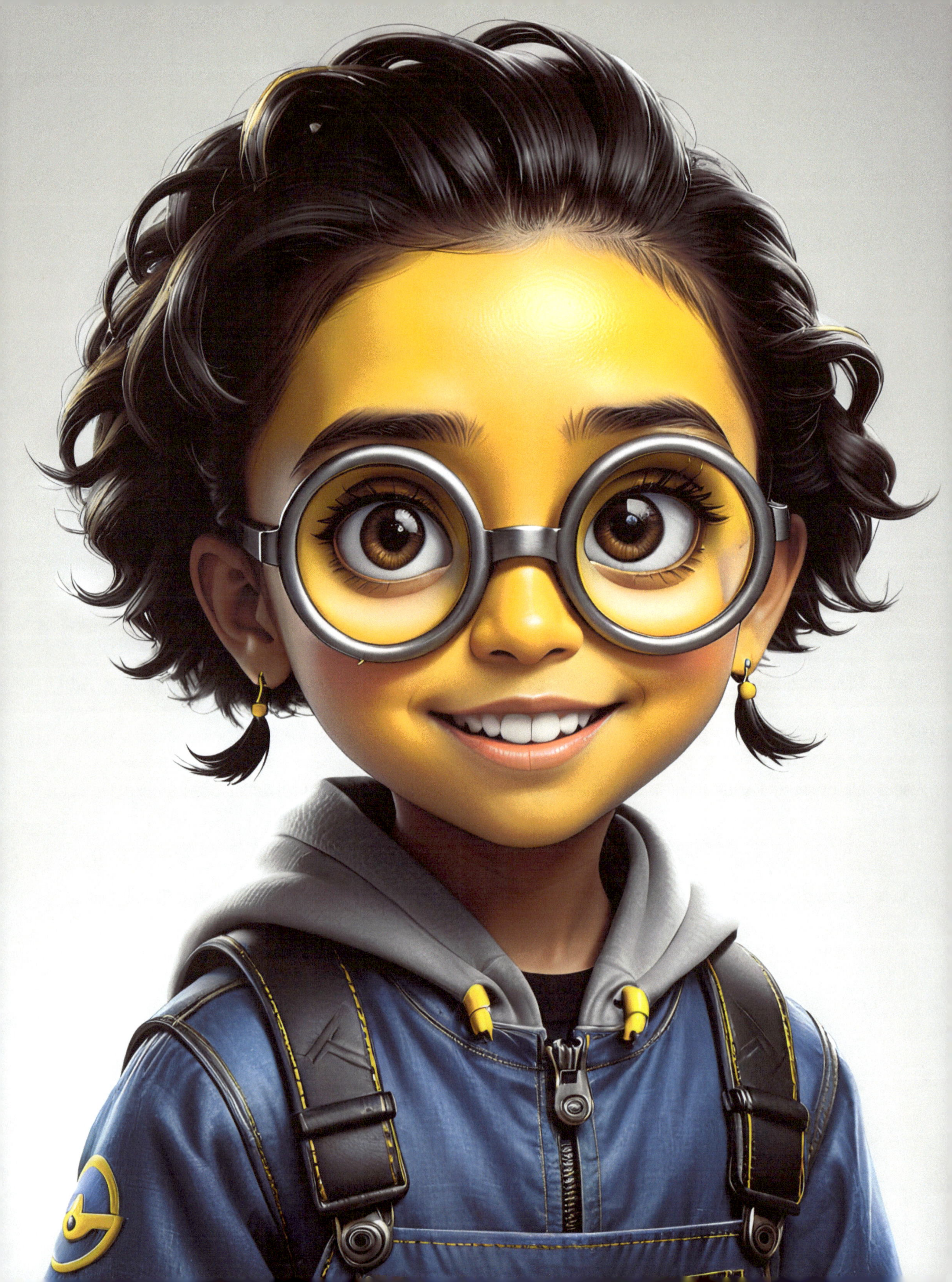

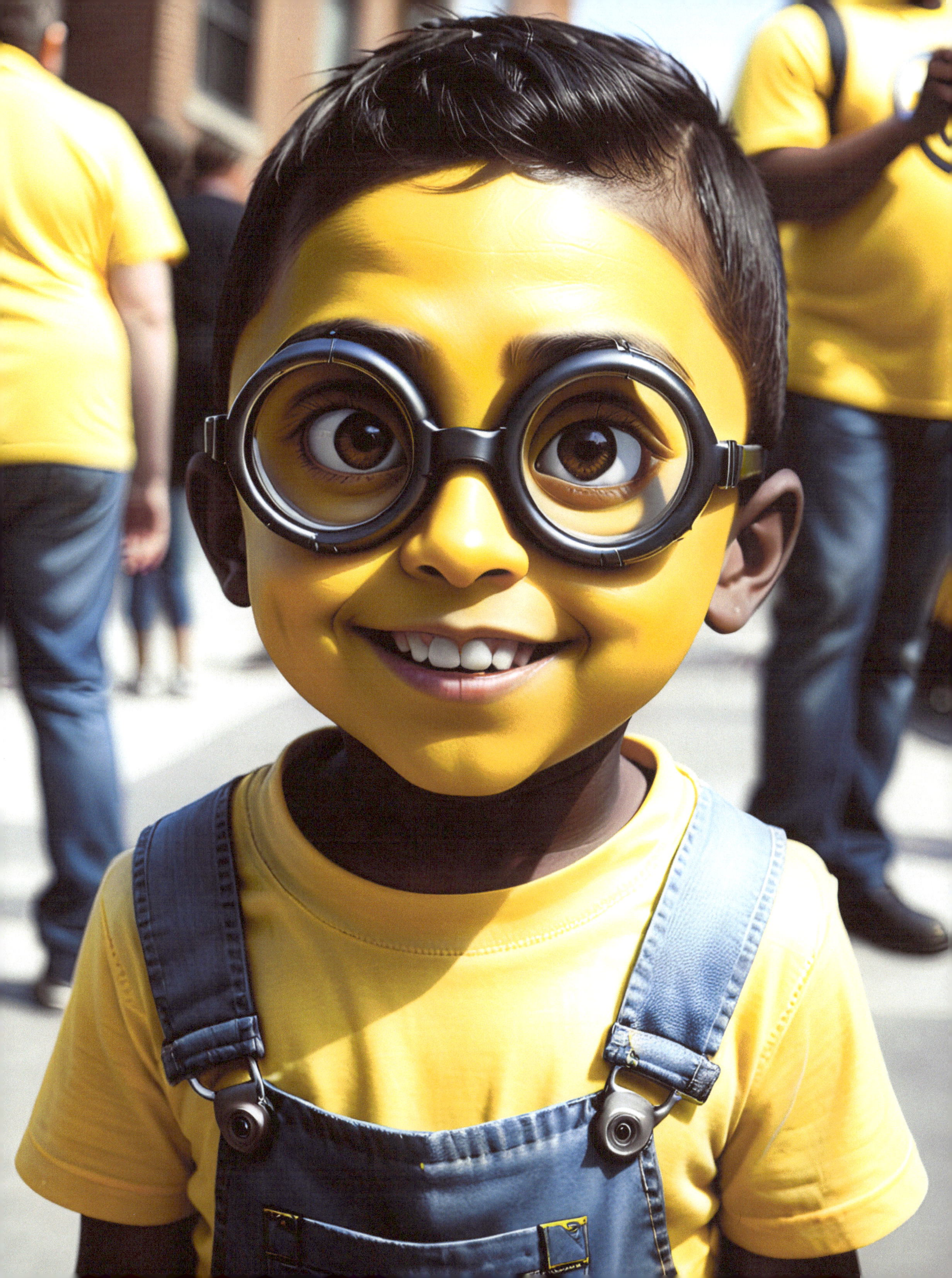

Face Painting Instructions: Snowman Theme – Step by Step

Tools and Materials:

Face paints: white, orange, blue

Brushes: thin and medium

Sponge

Bowl of water

Tissues and paper towels

Mirror

Step 1: Prepare the Skin

Wash and dry the child's face.

Step 2: Apply the White Base

Use a sponge to apply white paint over the entire face, creating a uniform base. Let it dry.

Step 3: Draw the Orange Nose

Use a medium brush and orange paint to draw a carrot-shaped nose on the child's nose. Let it dry.

Step 4: Add Blue and White Snowflakes

Use a thin brush and white and blue paint to draw snowflakes on the cheeks and forehead. Ensure the snowflakes are of various sizes and shapes to look natural.

Add small white dots around the snowflakes to create a snow effect.

Step 5: Add Details

Use a thin brush to add small accents around the nose and snowflakes, giving the design a more three-dimensional look.

You can add a light pink tint on the cheeks to give a healthy, wintery appearance.

Step 6: Finishing Touches

Ensure all lines are clear and the colors are well filled in. Show the child the final design in a mirror.

Step 7: Clean Up

Wash brushes and sponges with warm, soapy water. Test paints on a small skin area before painting.

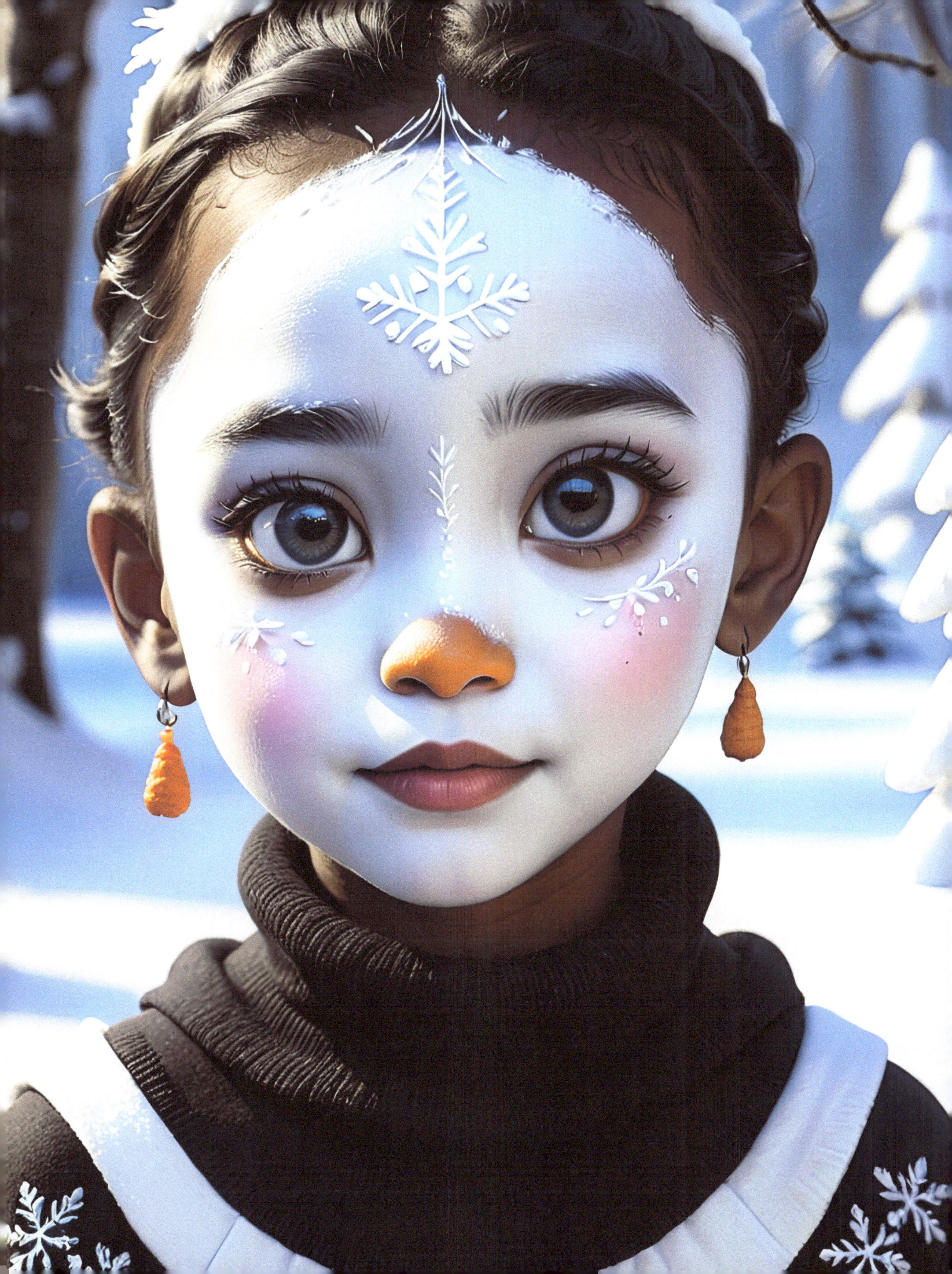

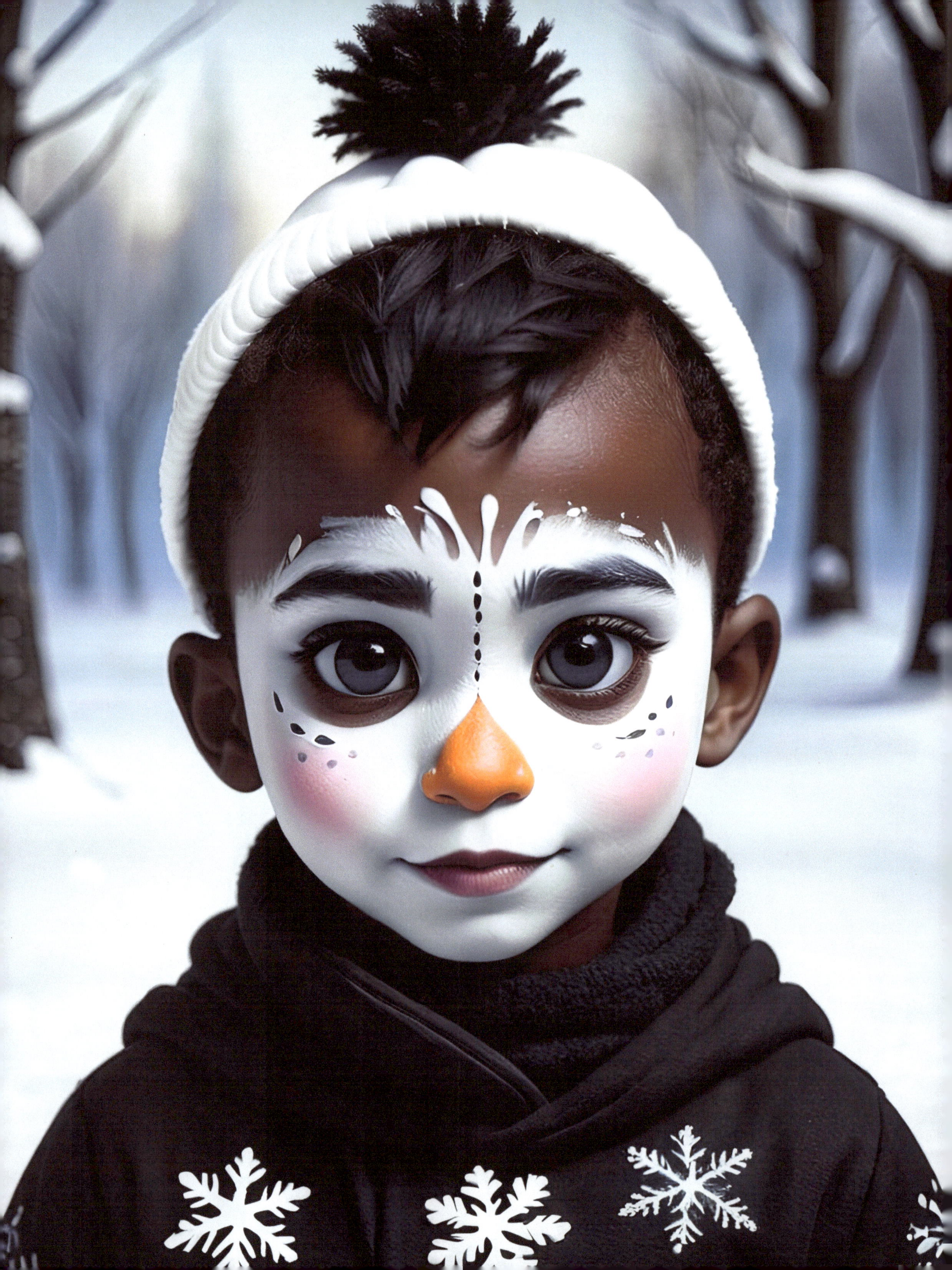

Face Painting Instructions: Tiger Design – Step by Step

Tools and Materials:

Face paints: orange, white, and black

Brushes: thin and medium

Sponge

Bowl of water

Tissues and paper towels

Mirror

Step 1: Prepare the Skin

Wash and dry the child's face.

Step 2: Apply the Base

Use a sponge to apply orange paint over the entire face, leaving the areas around the eyes and mouth white. Let it dry.

Step 3: Add White Elements

Use a sponge to apply white paint around the eyes, on the cheeks, nose, and chin. Let it dry.

Step 4: Draw the Outlines and Stripes

Use a thin brush and black paint to draw stripes on the forehead, cheeks, and around the eyes. Add outlines around the white areas on the nose and mouth.

Step 5: Fill in the Nose and Whiskers

Use a thin brush to paint the nose black. Add black dots on the white areas around the mouth and draw whiskers.

Step 6: Add Details

Add black stripes on the orange parts of the face to give a more realistic tiger look. Add white dots near the black stripes for extra effect.

Step 7: Finishing Touches

Ensure all lines are clear and the colors are well filled in. Show the child the final design in a mirror.

Step 8: Clean Up

Wash brushes and sponges with warm, soapy water. Test paints on a small skin area before painting.

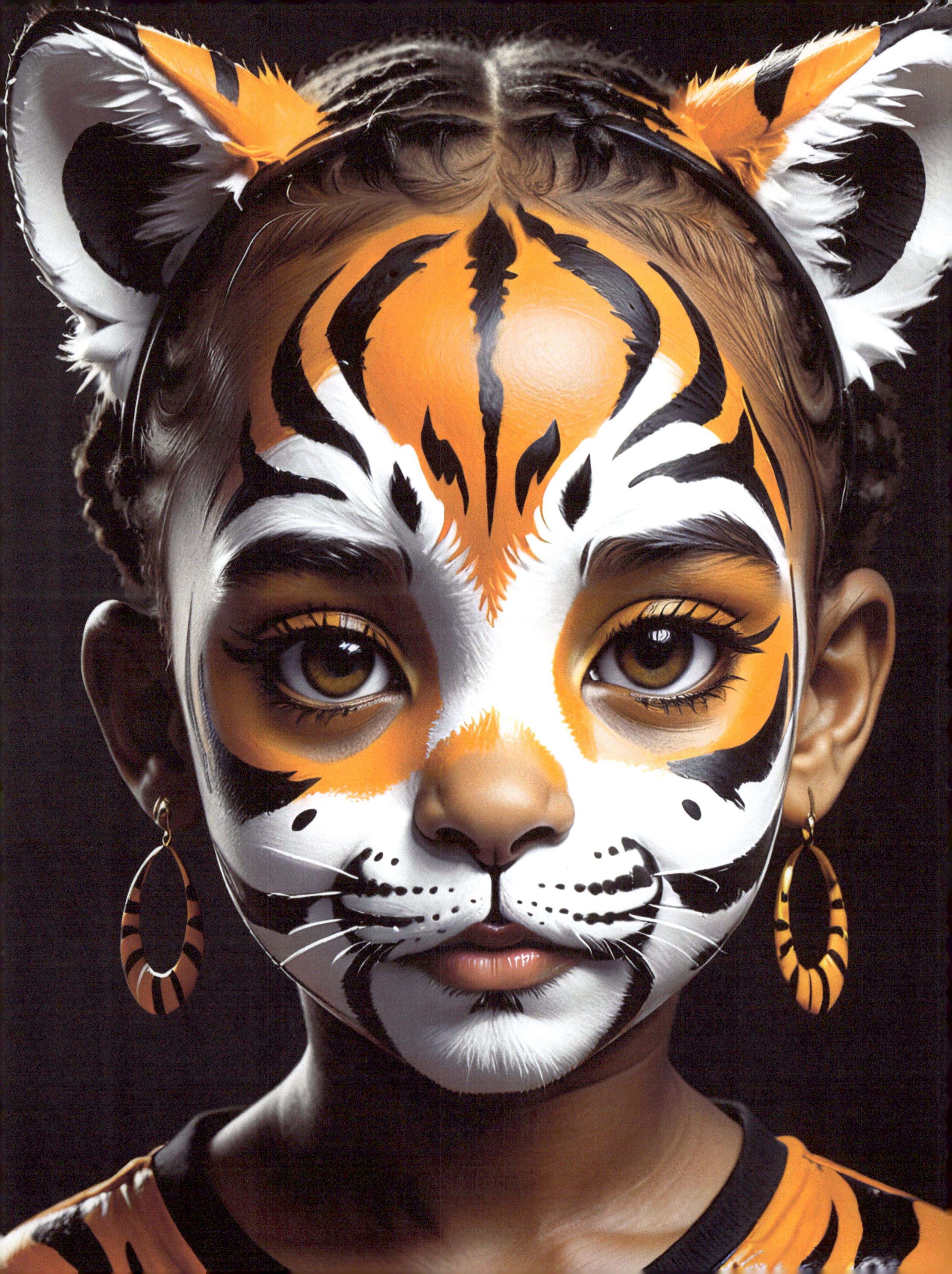

Face Painting Instructions: Pink Cat Theme – Step by Step

Tools and Materials:

Face paints: white, pink, black

Brushes: thin and medium

Sponge

Bowl of water

Tissues and paper towels

Mirror

Step 1: Prepare the Skin

Wash and dry the child's face.

Step 2: Apply White Spots

Use a medium brush or sponge to apply white paint on the child's cheeks, creating large round spots. Let it dry.

Step 3: Add Pink Accents

Use a thin brush and pink paint to add pink accents on the white spots on the cheeks. Let it dry.

Step 4: Draw Black Details

Use a thin brush and black paint to draw whiskers coming out from the white spots on the cheeks. Add small black dots on the white spots to create the cat's nose and mouth.

Step 5: Add White Droplets

Use a thin brush and white paint to add small white droplets around the eyes and on the nose for extra effect.

Step 6: Finishing Touches

Ensure all lines are clear and the colors are well filled in. Show the child the final design in a mirror.

Step 7: Clean Up

Wash brushes and sponges with warm, soapy water. Test paints on a small skin area before painting.

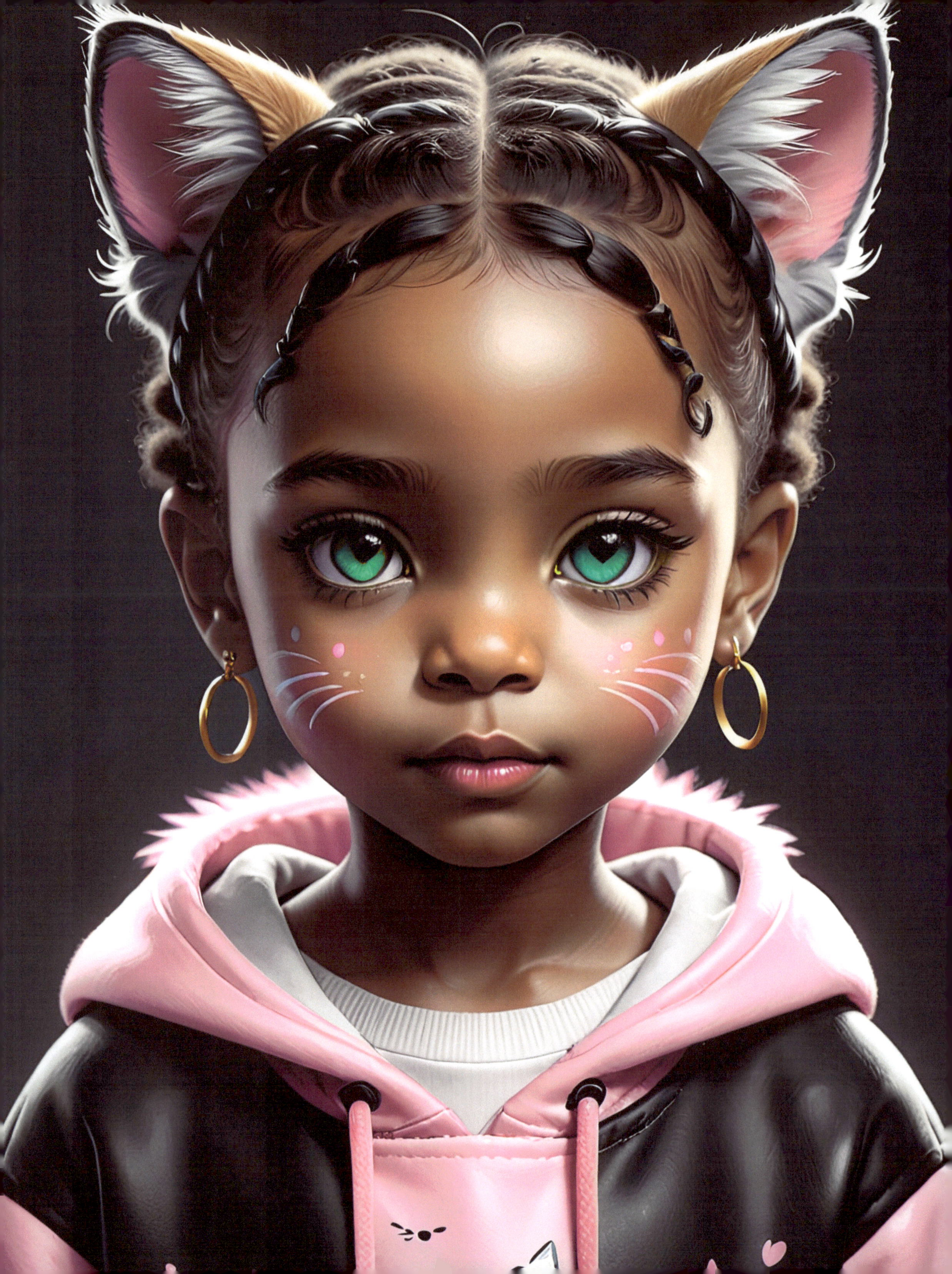

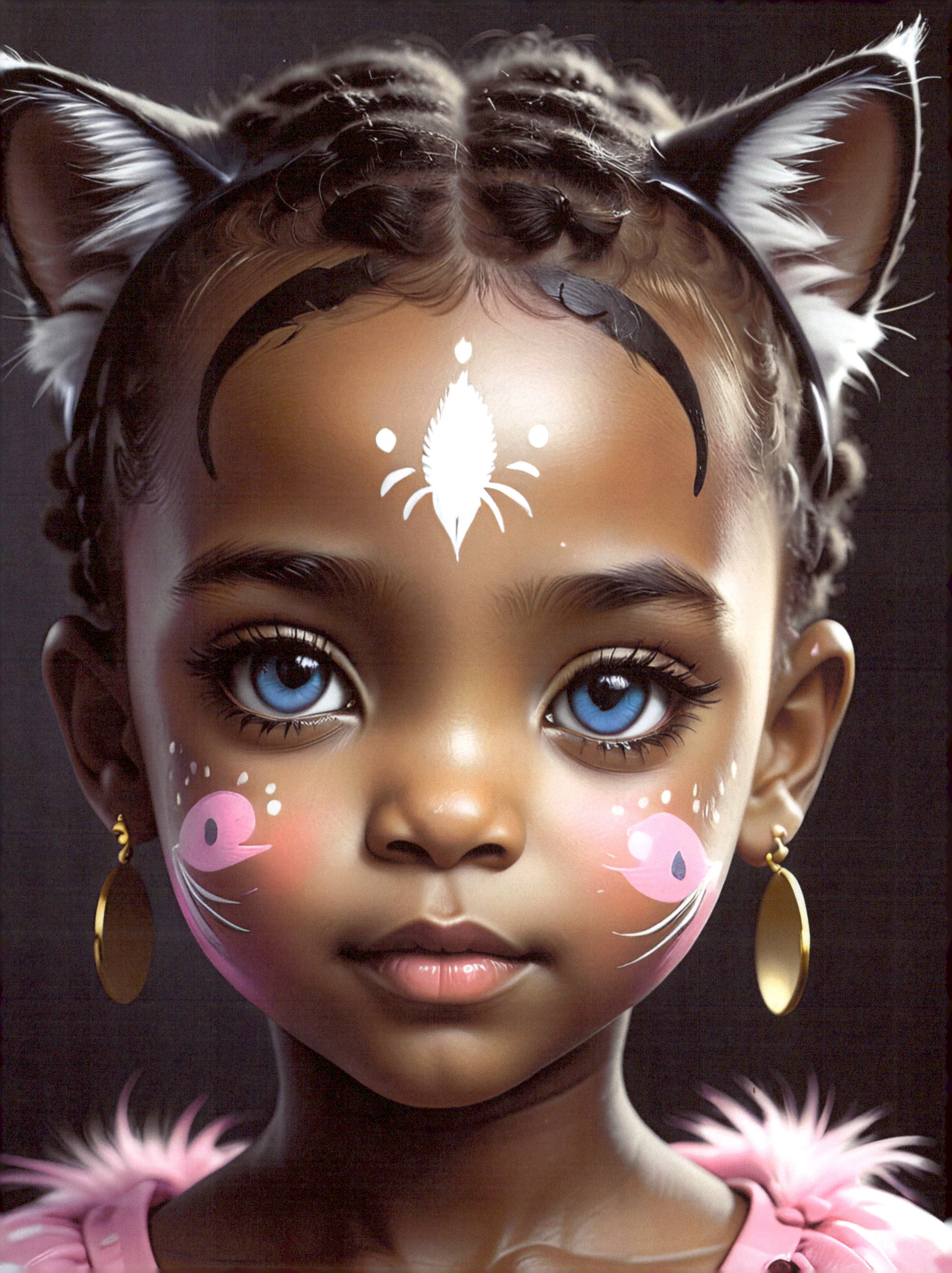

FFace Painting Instructions: Black Cat Theme – Step by Step

Tools and Materials:

Face paints: black, pink, white

Brushes: thin and medium

Sponge

Bowl of water

Tissues and paper towels

Mirror

Headband with cat ears

Step 1: Prepare the Skin

Wash and dry the child's face.

Step 2: Apply Black Areas

Use a sponge to apply black paint around the eyes, nose, and cheeks, creating a cat mask shape. Let it dry.

Step 3: Draw Details

Use a thin brush and black paint to draw the contours around the nose and mouth.

Step 4: Add Pink Accents

Use a thin brush and pink paint to color the tip of the nose and lips.

Step 5: Add White Details

Use a thin brush and white paint to add whiskers and dots on the cheeks.

Step 6: Add Pink Accents to the Mask

Add pink accents around the eyes to highlight the mask. You can add a few pink stripes for contrast.

Step 7: Finishing Touches

Ensure all lines are clear and the colors are well filled in. Show the child the final design in a mirror.

Step 8: Put on the Cat Ear Headband

Place the headband with cat ears on the child's head to complete the look.

Step 9: Clean Up

Wash brushes and sponges with warm, soapy water. Test paints on a small skin area before painting.

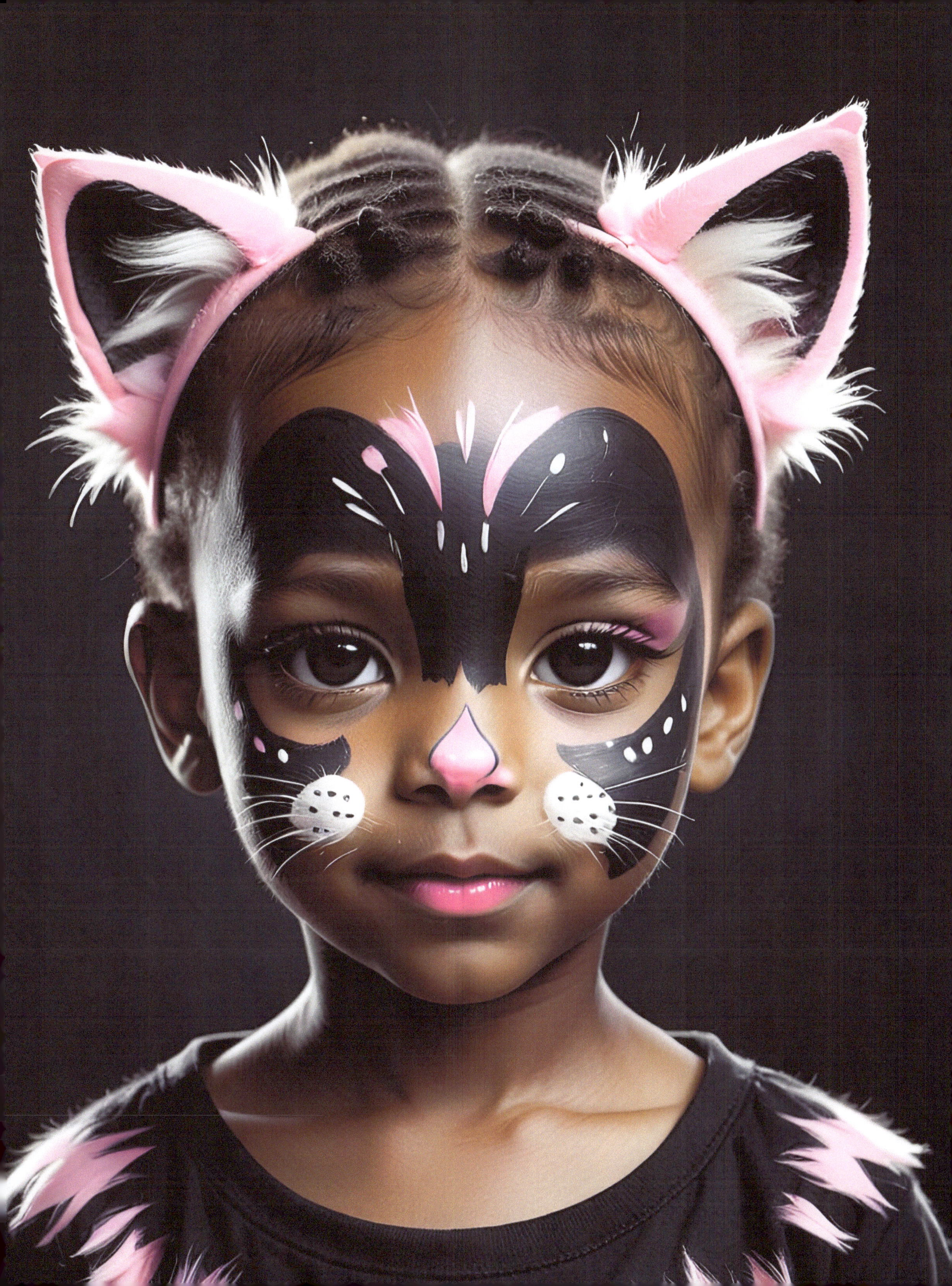

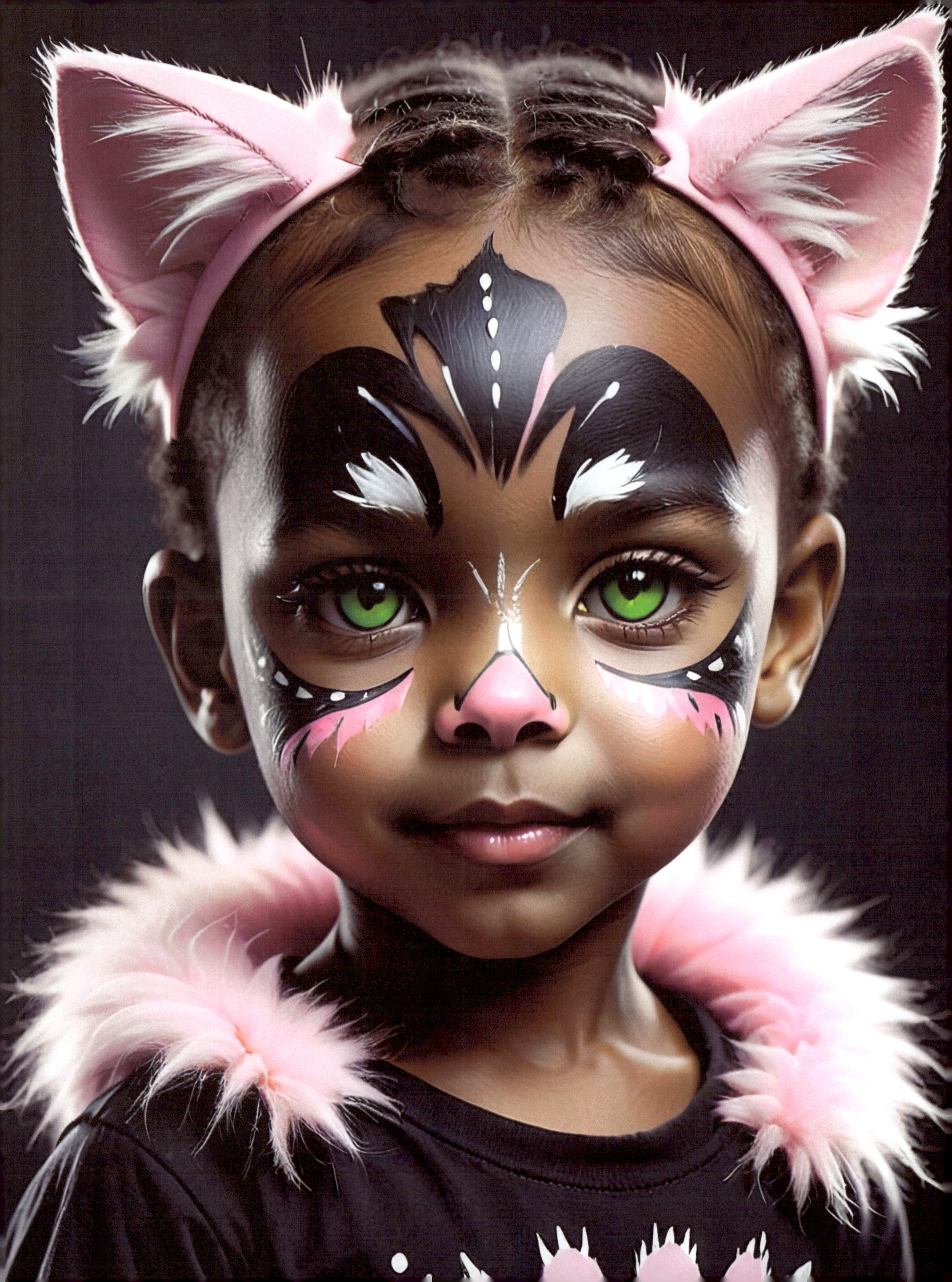

Face Painting Instructions: Panda Theme – Step by Step

Tools and Materials:

Face paints: white, black

Brushes: thin and medium

Sponge

Bowl of water

Tissues and paper towels

Mirror

Step 1: Prepare the Skin

Wash and dry the child's face.

Step 2: Apply the White Base

Use a sponge to apply white paint over the entire face, except for the areas around the eyes. Let it dry.

Step 3: Draw Black Circles Around the Eyes

Use a medium brush and black paint to draw large circles around the eyes, resembling the panda's distinctive "glasses". Let it dry.

Step 4: Draw the Black Nose

Use a thin brush to draw a small black triangular nose on the tip of the child's nose.

Step 5: Add Details

Use a thin brush to add small black dots on the upper lip, creating whiskers.

You can add a pink tint on the cheeks to give the panda a cute look.

Step 6: Finishing Touches

Ensure all lines are clear and the colors are well filled in. Show the child the final design in a mirror.

Step 7: Clean Up

Wash brushes and sponges with warm, soapy water. Test paints on a small skin area before painting.

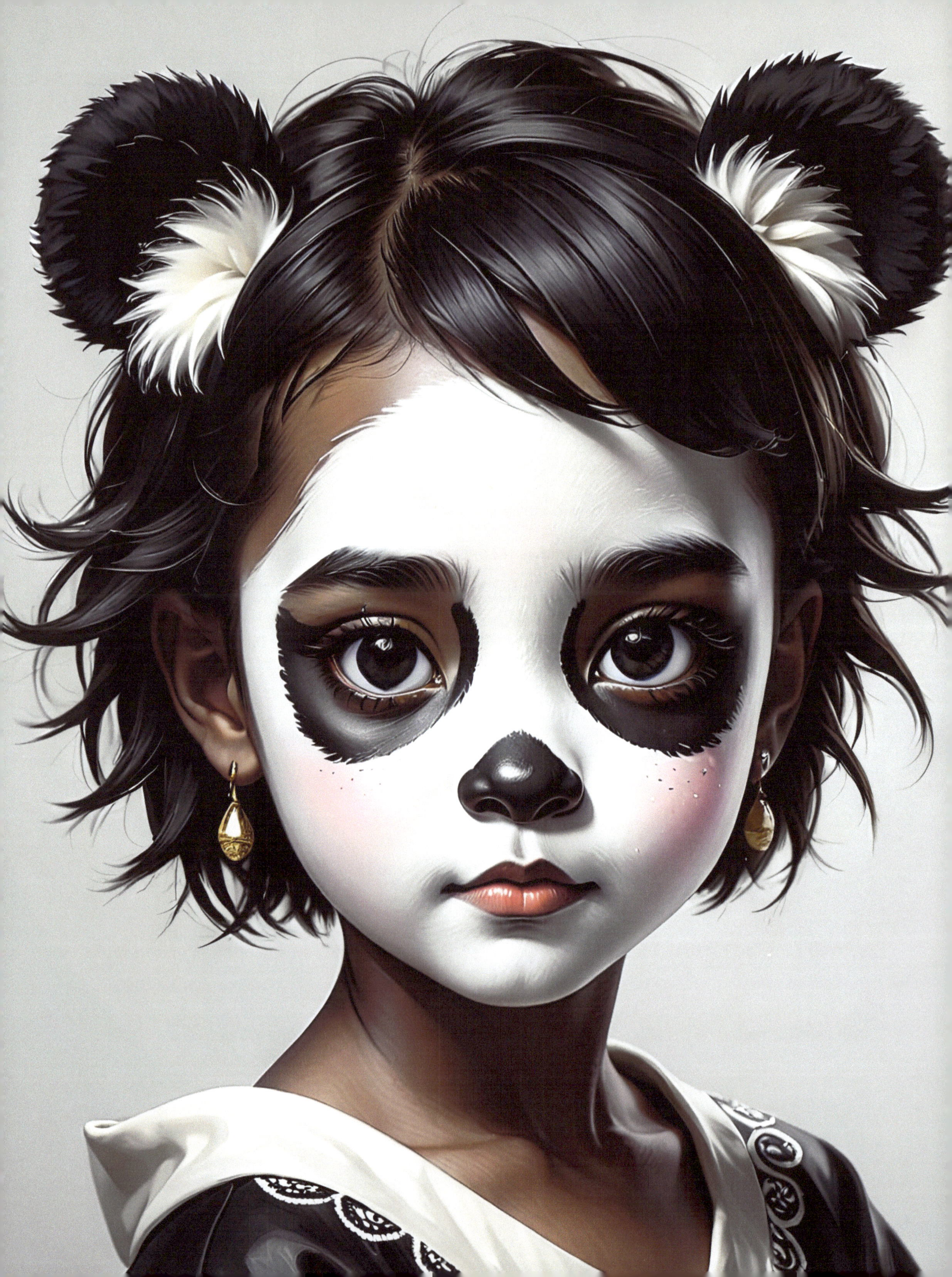

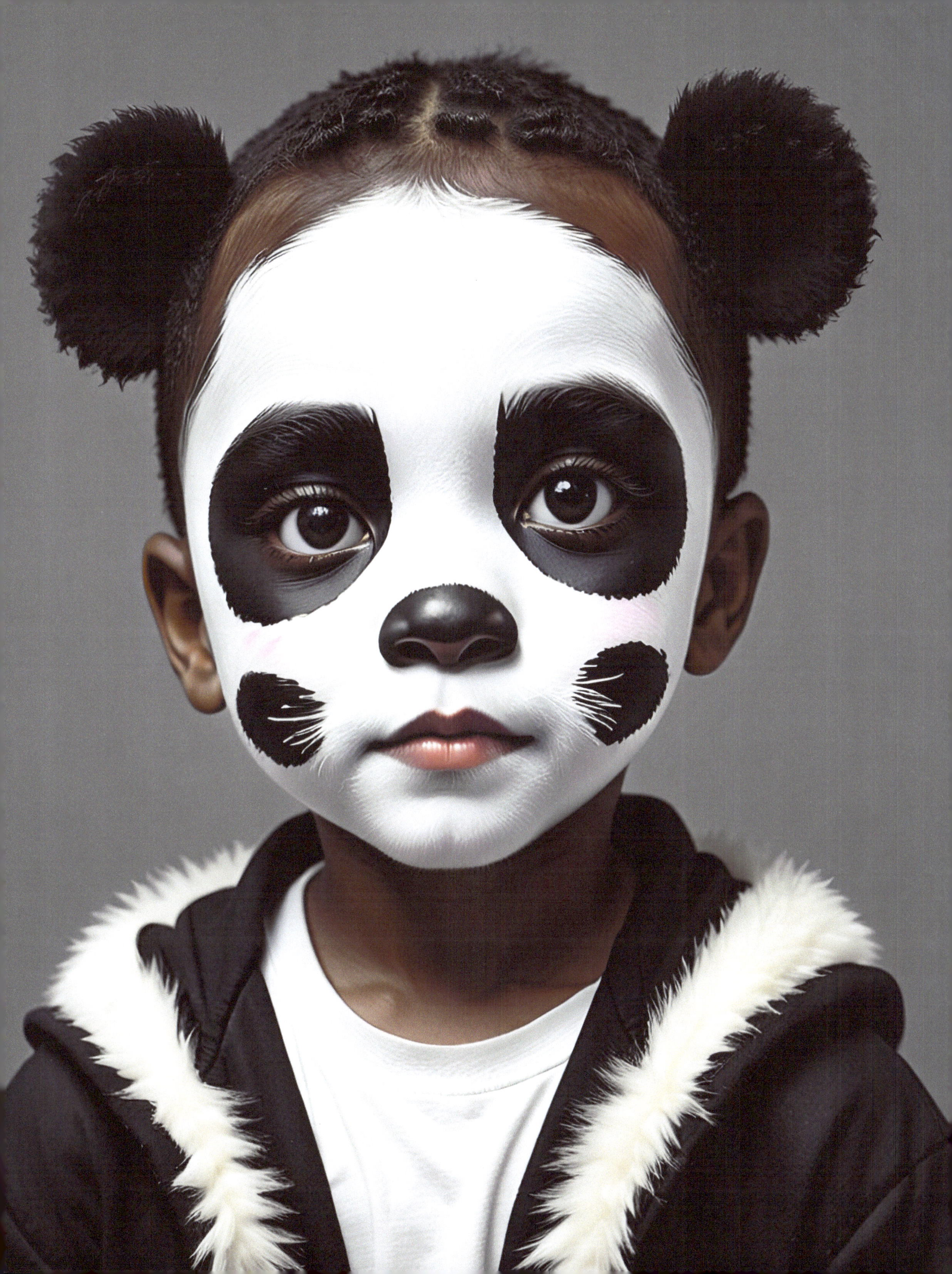

Face Painting Instructions: Lion Theme — Step by Step

Tools and Materials:

Face paints: yellow, orange, black

Brushes: thin and medium

Sponge

Bowl of water

Tissues and paper towels

Mirror

Step 1: Prepare the Skin

Wash and dry the child's face.

Step 2: Apply the Yellow Base

Use a sponge to apply yellow paint on the forehead, cheeks, and nose. Let it dry.

Step 3: Add Orange Accents

Use a sponge to apply orange paint in the center of the forehead and nose, creating a gradient effect with the yellow. Let it dry.

Step 4: Draw Black Details

Use a thin brush and black paint to draw diamond shapes in the center of the forehead and small stripes on the cheeks to resemble the lion's mane.

Add small black dots on the cheeks to create the effect of fur.

Step 5: Add Shadows and Finishing Touches

Use a thin brush to add black accents around the yellow and orange areas, giving them depth and definition. Add details on the forehead and around the eyes to create a more realistic lion look.

Step 6: Finishing Touches

Ensure all lines are clear and the colors are well filled in. Show the child the final design in a mirror.

Step 7: Clean Up

Wash brushes and sponges with warm, soapy water. Test paints on a small skin area before painting.

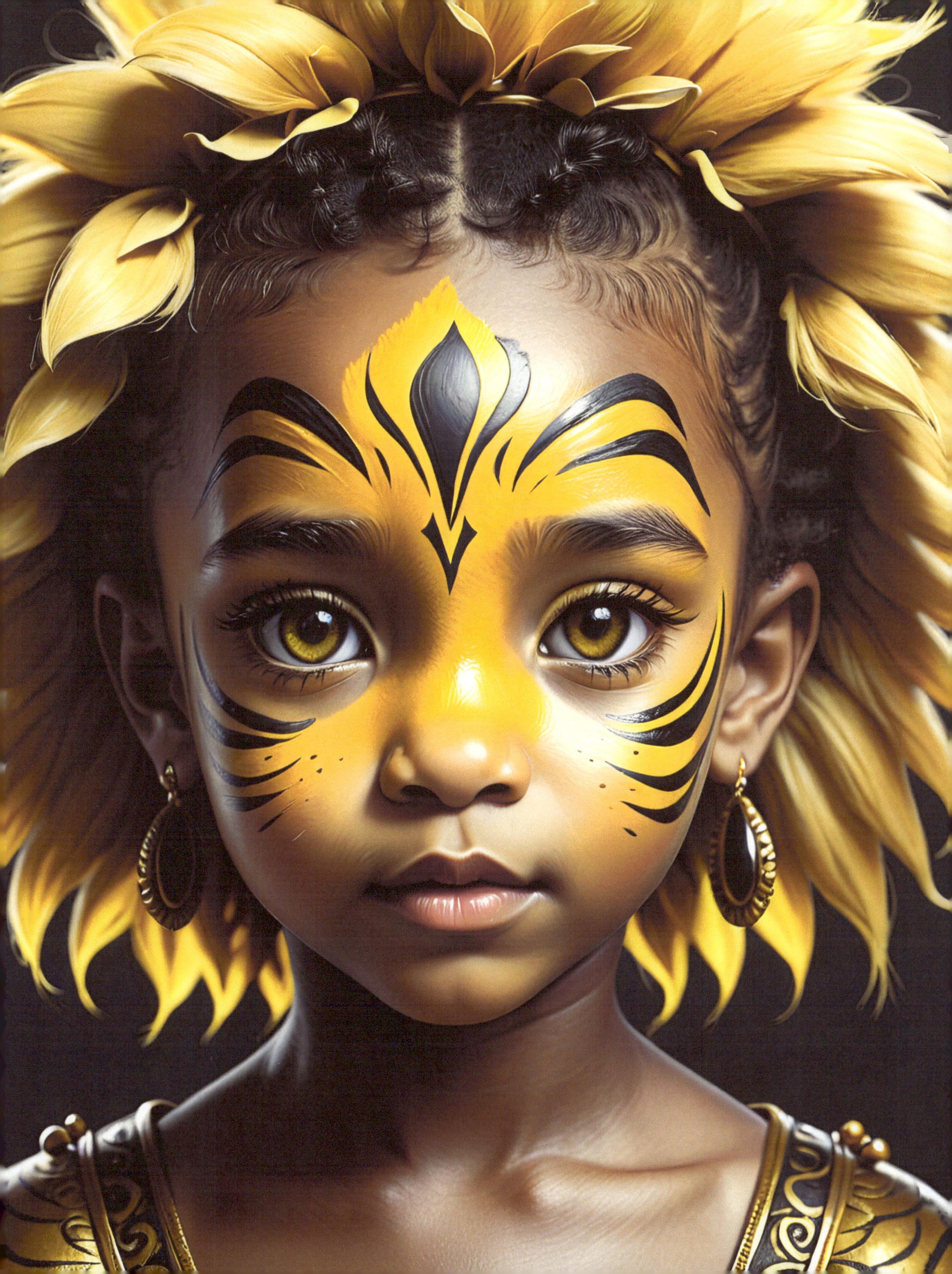

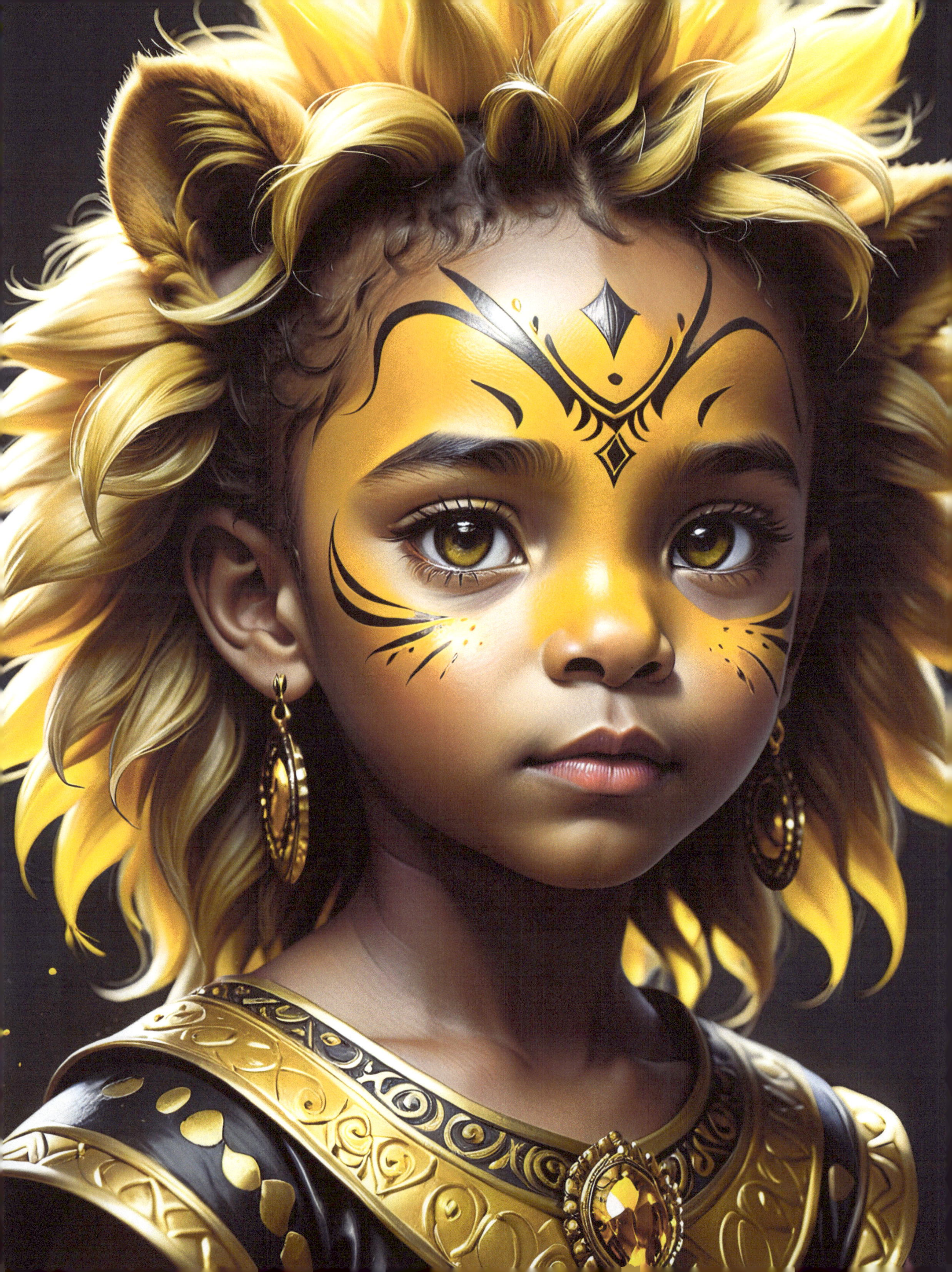

Tools and Materials:

Face paints: white, pink, black

Brushes: thin and medium

Sponge

Bowl of water

Tissues and paper towels

Mirror

Step 1: Prepare the Skin

Wash and dry the child's face.

Step 2: Apply the White Base

Use a sponge to apply white paint to the central part of the face, covering the forehead, cheeks, nose, and chin, creating a mask–like shape. Let it dry.

Step 3: Add Pink Accents

Use a sponge or medium brush to apply pink paint to the cheeks and nose. Let it dry.

Step 4: Draw Black Details

Use a thin brush and black paint to draw whiskers extending from the pink cheeks.

Add small black dots above the whiskers for a realistic look.

Draw black lines on the top of the white area above the eyes to add fur–like details.

Step 5: Add White Details

Use a thin brush and white paint to add small white dots around the eyes and on the tip of the nose for extra effect.

Step 6: Finishing Touches

Ensure all lines are clear and the colors are well filled in. Show the child the final design in a mirror.

Step 7: Clean Up

Wash brushes and sponges with warm, soapy water. Test paints on a small skin area before painting.

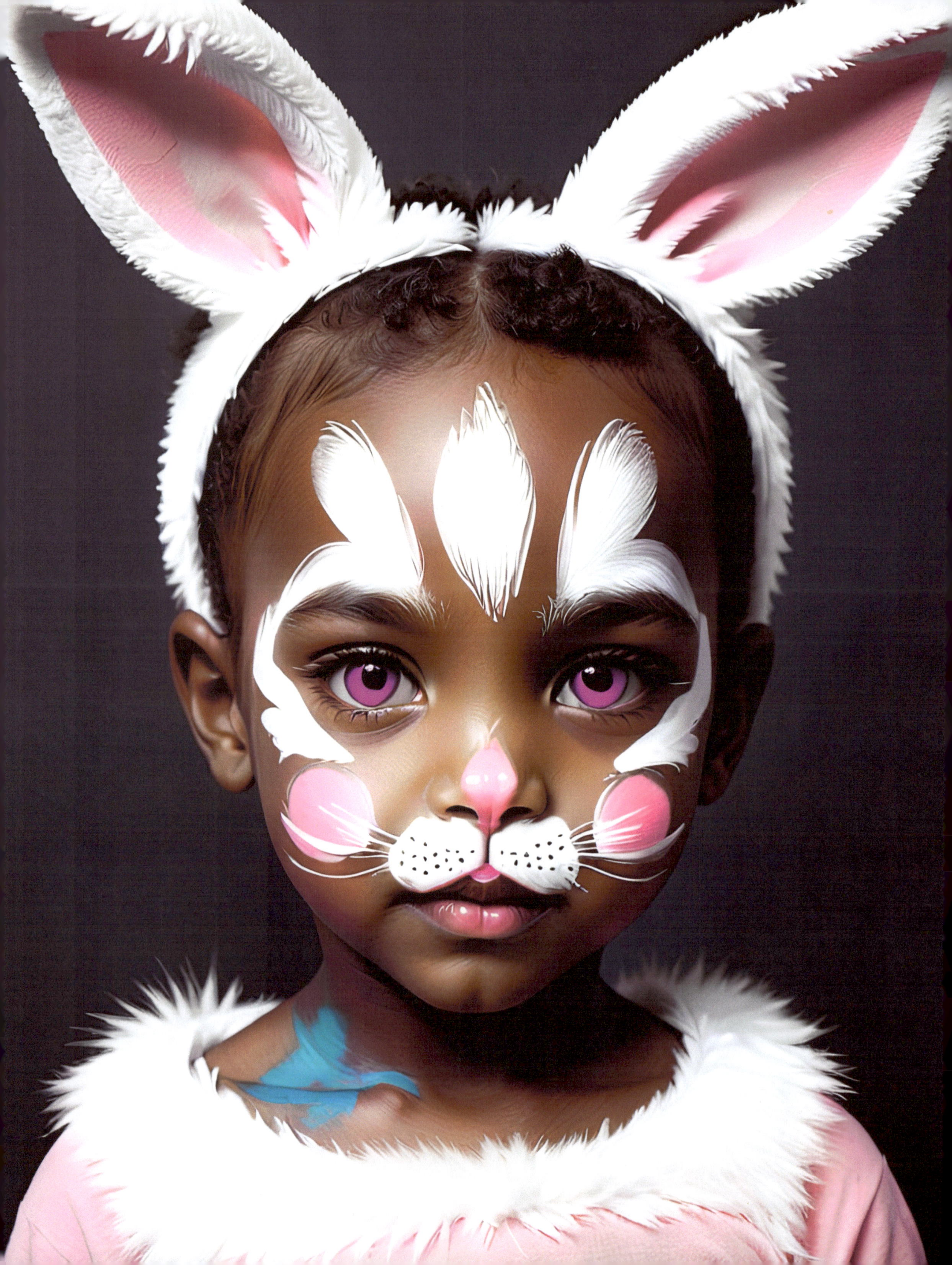

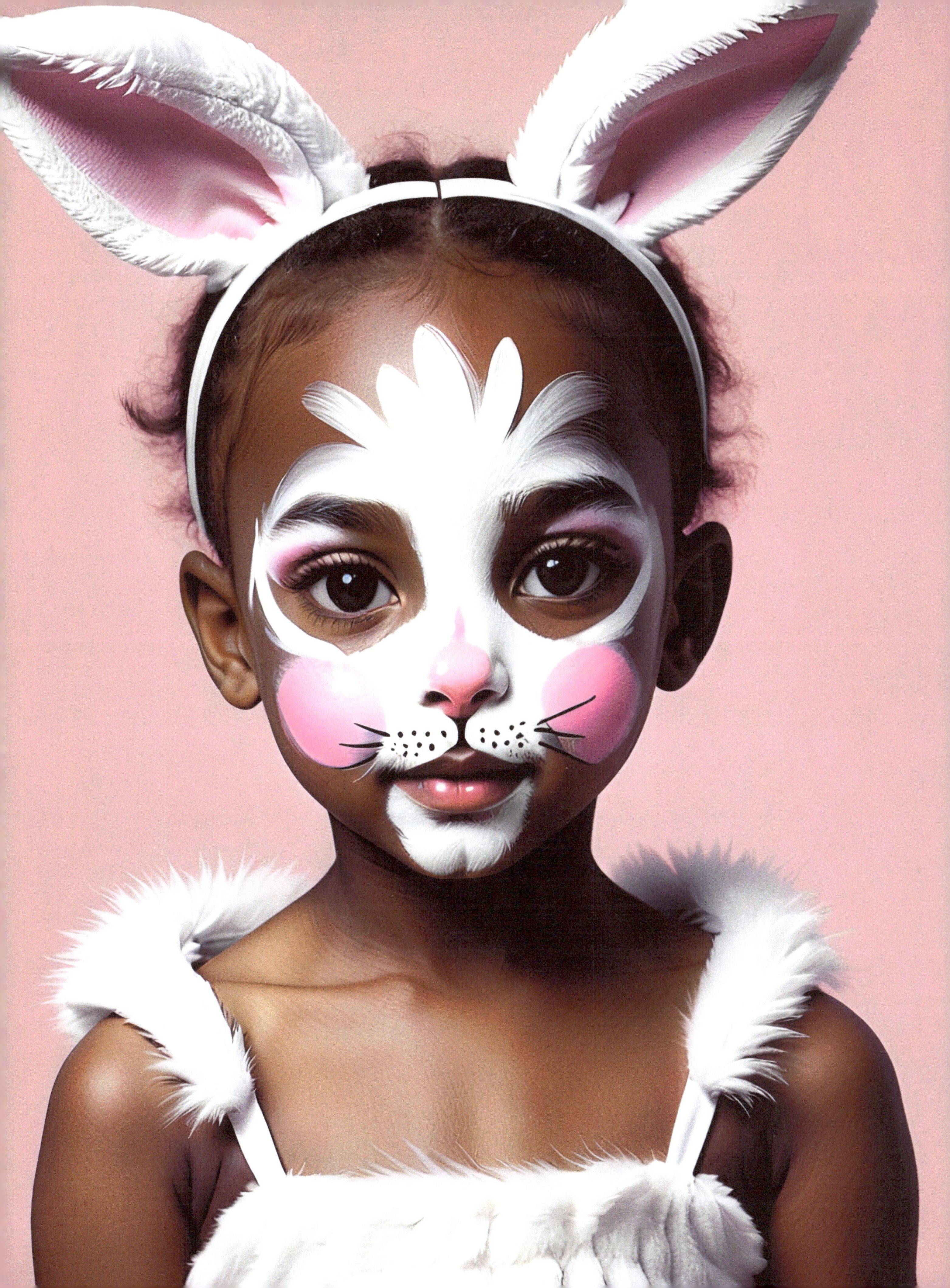

Face Painting Instructions: Zebra Theme – Step by Step

Tools and Materials:

Face paints: white, black

Brushes: thin and medium

Sponge

Bowl of water

Tissues and paper towels

Mirror

Step 1: Prepare the Skin

Wash and dry the child's face.

Step 2: Apply the White Base

Use a sponge to apply white paint over the entire face. Let it dry.

Step 3: Draw the Black Stripes

Use a thin brush and black paint to draw vertical and diagonal stripes on the forehead, cheeks, and nose, mimicking the zebra's stripe pattern.

Start from the forehead, drawing a central shape resembling an inverted diamond. Then add stripes extending outward.

Step 4: Add Stripes on Cheeks and Nose

Continue drawing stripes on the cheeks, extending from the nose outward.

Add small stripes on both sides of the nose for a realistic zebra look.

Step 5: Add Details

Add small black dots on the cheeks for extra effect.

You can add a few thin stripes around the eyes to emphasize the zebra pattern.

Step 6: Finishing Touches

Ensure all lines are clear and the colors are well filled in. Show the child the final design in a mirror.

Step 7: Clean Up

Wash brushes and sponges with warm, soapy water. Test paints on a small skin area before painting.

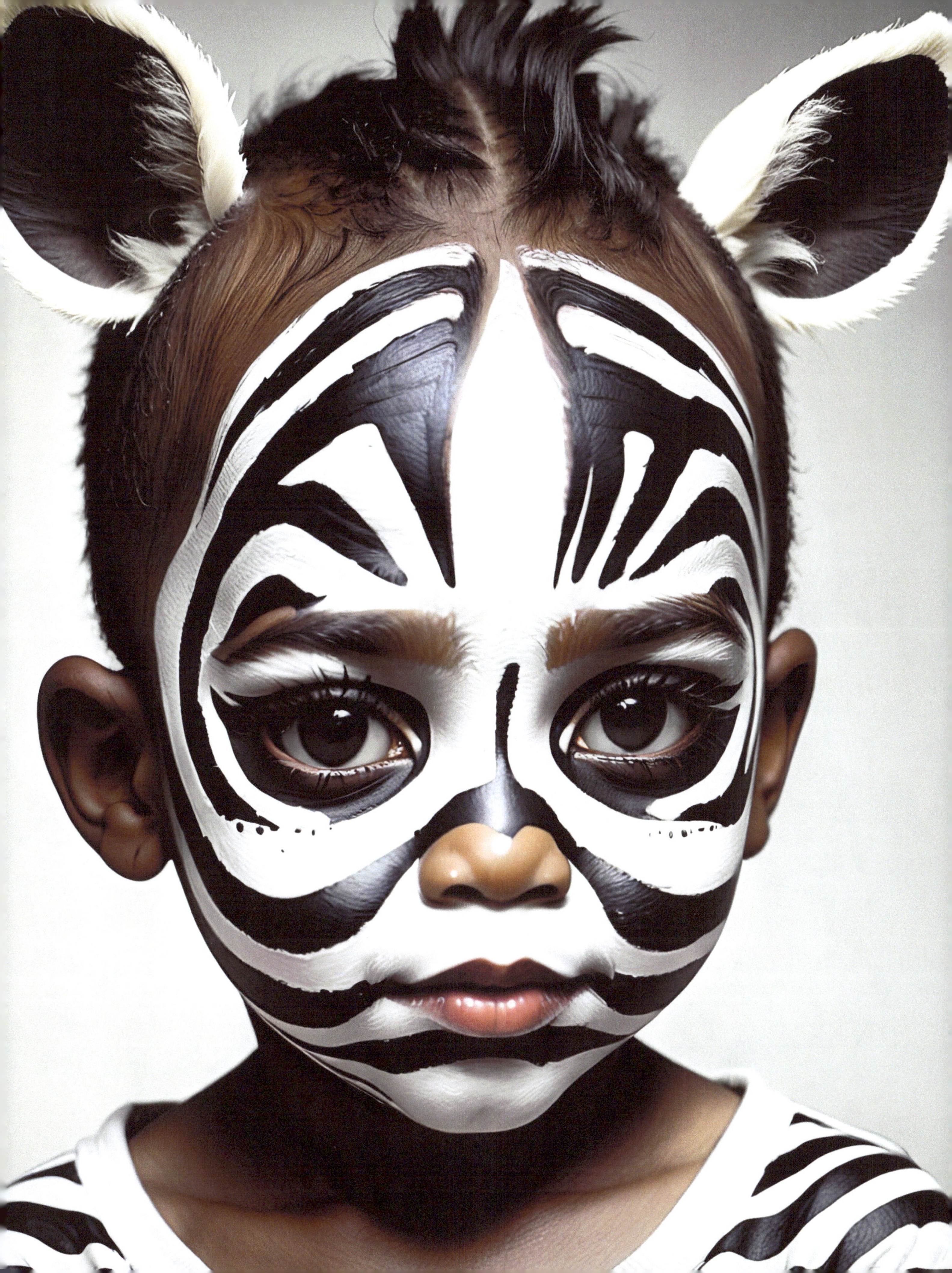

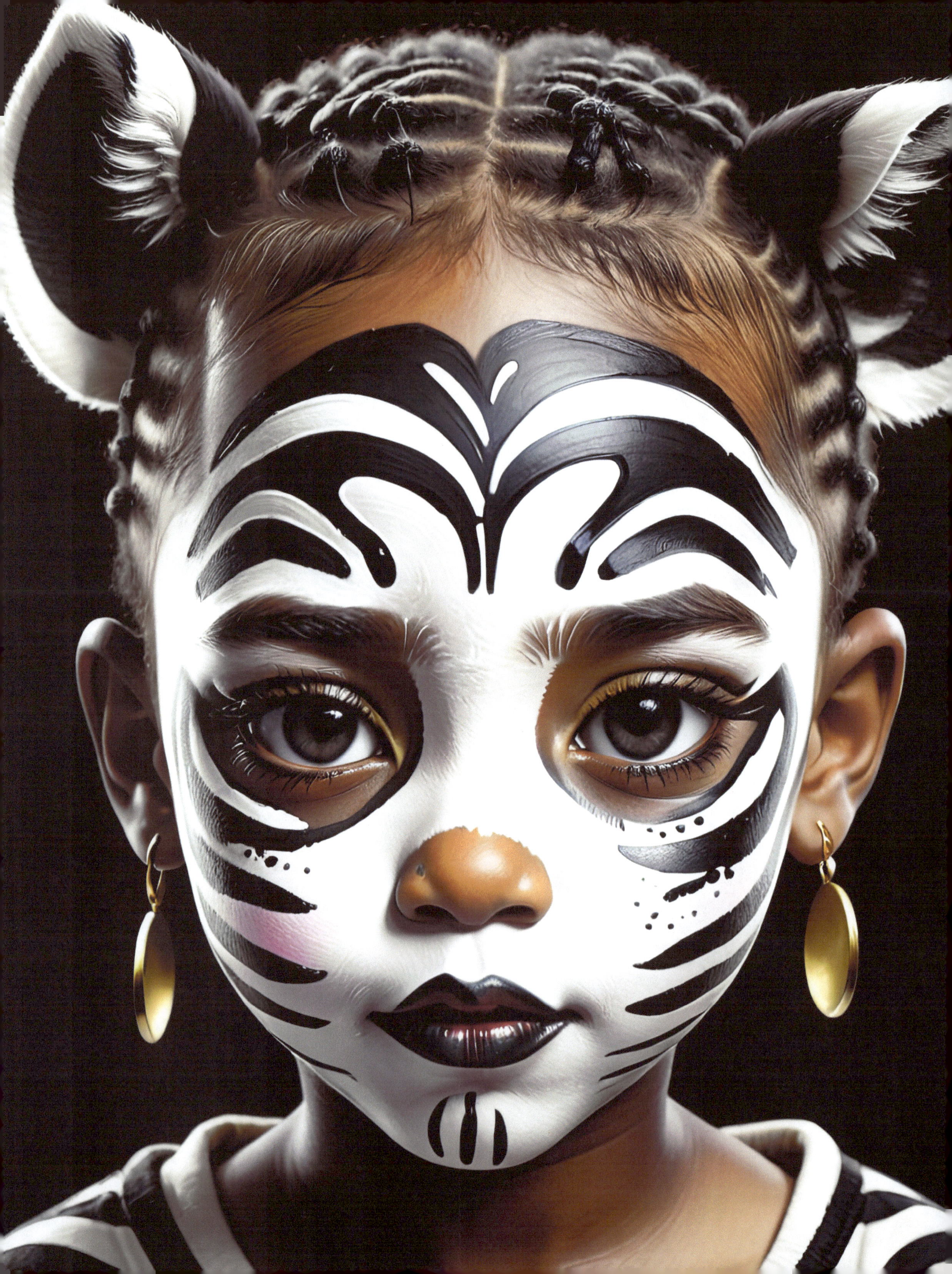

Face Painting Instructions: Giraffe Theme — Step by Step

Tools and Materials:

Face paints: yellow, brown, black

Brushes: thin and medium

Sponge

Bowl of water

Tissues and paper towels

Mirror

Step 1: Prepare the Skin

Wash and dry the child's face.

Step 2: Apply the Yellow Base

Use a sponge to apply yellow paint on the forehead, nose, and cheeks, creating the main structure of the giraffe pattern. Let it dry.

Step 3: Draw Brown Spots

Use a thin brush and brown paint to draw irregular shapes of spots on the yellow area. The spots should be of various sizes and shapes to mimic the natural giraffe pattern.

Step 4: Add Details on Cheeks and Forehead

Use a thin brush to add small brown spots on the child's cheeks and a few additional spots on the forehead to complete the pattern.

Step 5: Draw the Black Nose

Use a thin brush and black paint to draw a small black nose on the tip of the child's nose.

Step 6: Add White Accents

Use a thin brush and white paint to add small white accents around the brown spots and on the nose for extra effect.

Step 7: Finishing Touches

Ensure all lines are clear and the colors are well filled in. Show the child the final design in a mirror.

Step 8: Clean Up

Wash brushes and sponges with warm, soapy water. Test paints on a small skin area before painting.

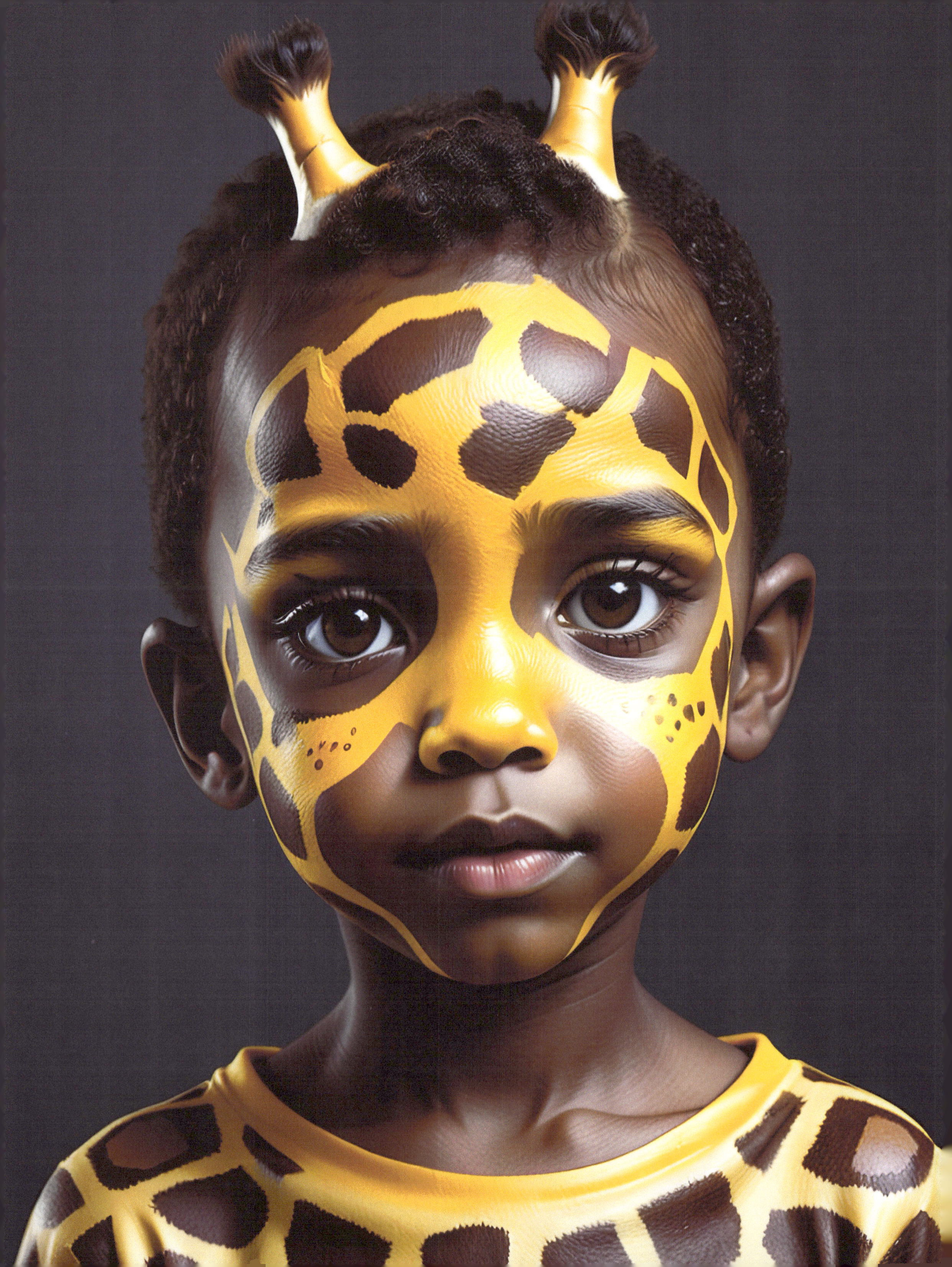

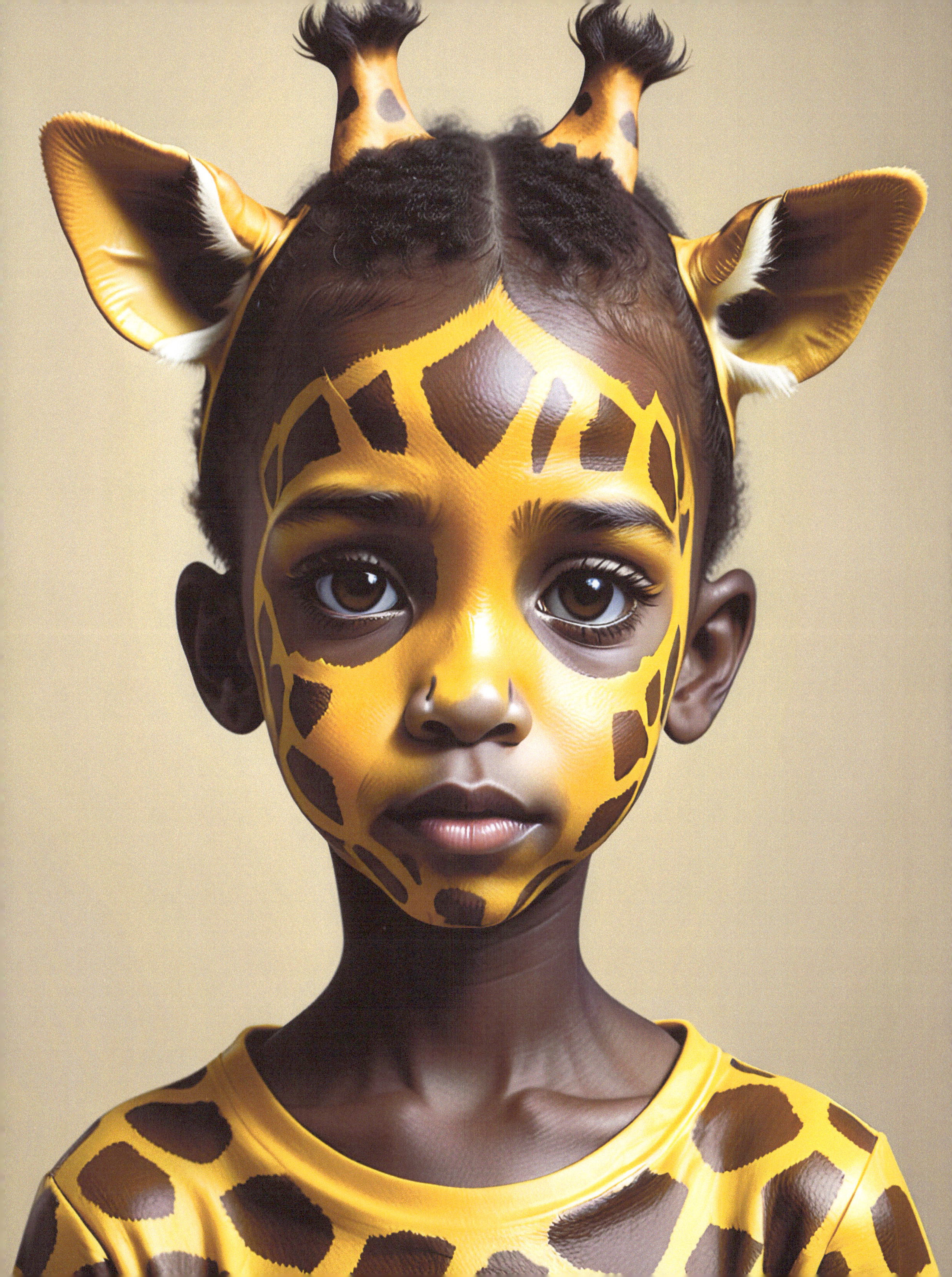

Face Painting Instructions: Bee Theme – Step by Step

Tools and Materials:

Face paints: yellow, black

Brushes: thin and medium

Sponge

Bowl of water

Tissues and paper towels

Mirror

Step 1: Prepare the Skin

Wash and dry the child's face.

Step 2: Apply the Yellow Base

Use a sponge to apply yellow paint on the forehead, cheeks, and nose, creating the main structure of the bee pattern. Let it dry.

Step 3: Draw Black Circles on Cheeks

Use a medium brush and black paint to draw black circles on both cheeks. In the center of each circle, add a small yellow dot to resemble the bee pattern.

Step 4: Draw Black Details

Use a thin brush and black paint to draw thin lines from the nose upward to the forehead, creating antennae shapes.

Add a few black stripes on the forehead and around the nose to add more details to the pattern.

Step 5: Draw the Black Nose

Use a thin brush and black paint to draw a small black nose on the tip of the child's nose.

Step 6: Add White Accents

Use a thin brush and white paint to add small white dots on the antennae and around the black nose for extra effect.

Step 7: Finishing Touches

Ensure all lines are clear and the colors are well filled in. Show the child the final design in a mirror.

Step 8: Clean Up

Wash brushes and sponges with warm, soapy water. Test paints on a small skin area before painting.

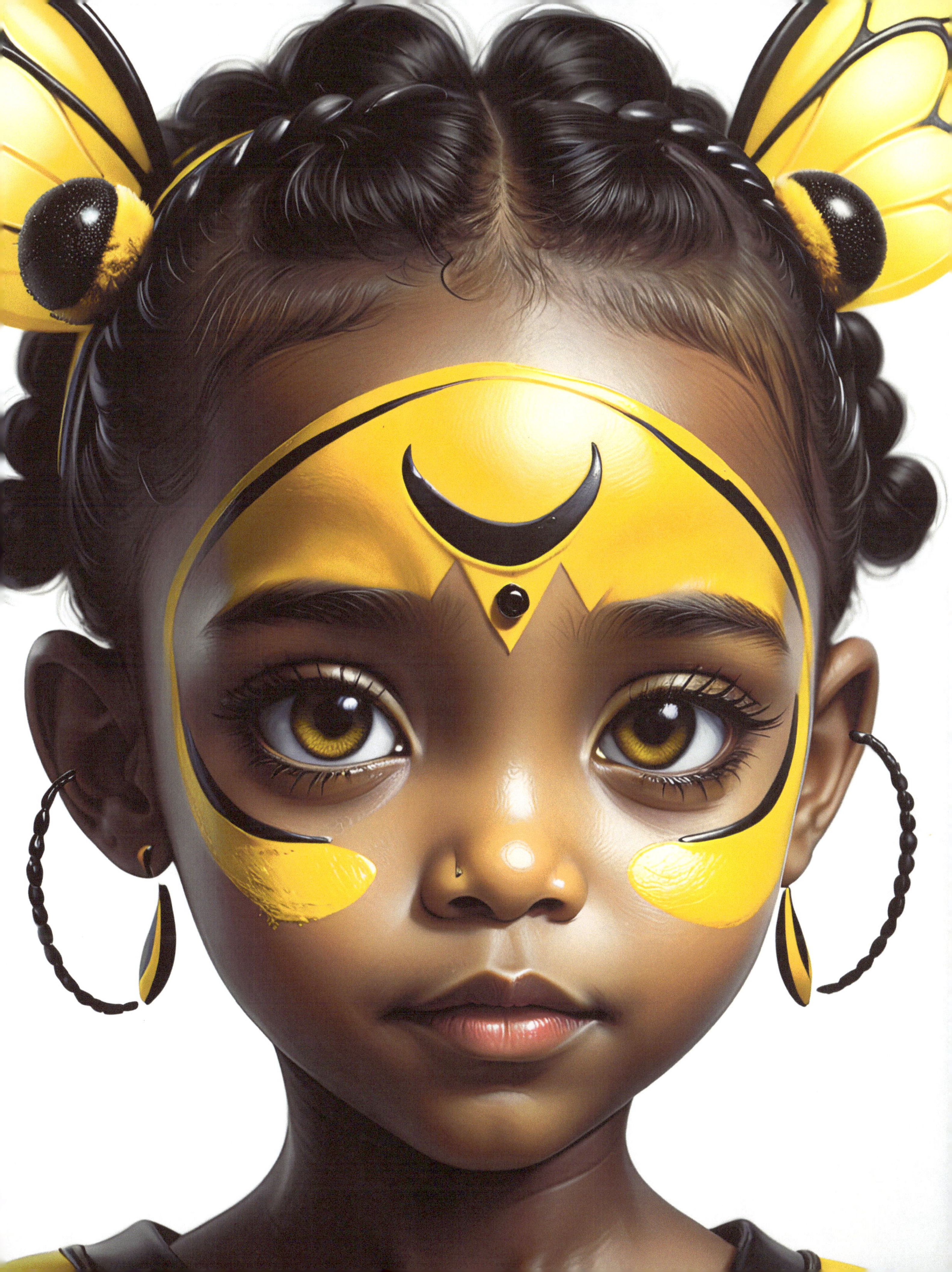

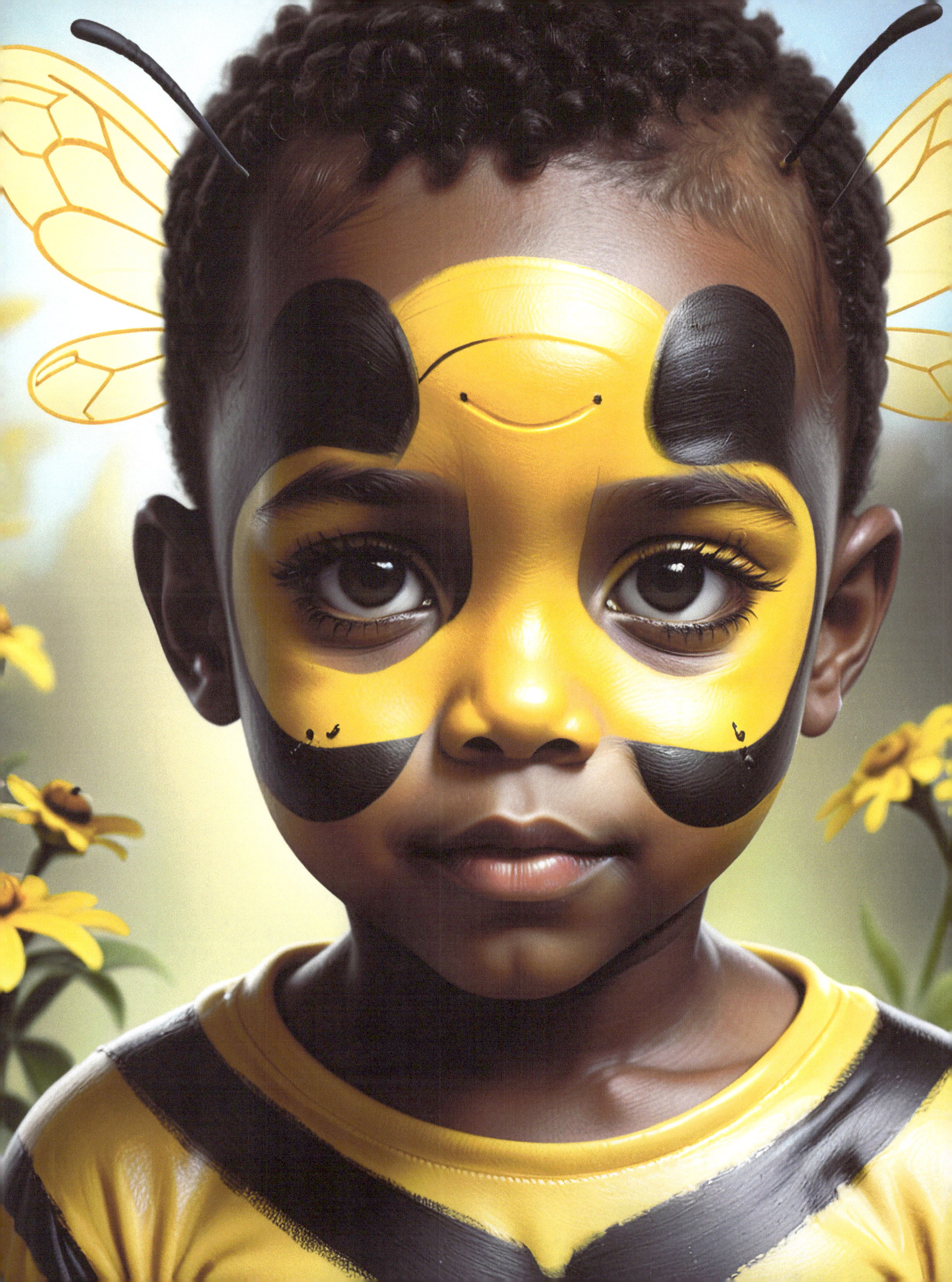

Face Painting Instructions: Fox Theme – Step by Step

Tools and Materials:

Face paints: orange, white, black

Brushes: thin and medium

Sponge

Bowl of water

Tissues and paper towels

Mirror

Step 1: Prepare the Skin

Wash and dry the child's face.

Step 2: Apply the Orange Base

Use a sponge to apply orange paint on the forehead, cheeks, and nose, creating the main structure of the fox pattern. Let it dry.

Step 3: Add White Accents

Use a medium brush and white paint to add white accents around the eyes, on the cheeks, and under the nose. Let it dry.

Step 4: Draw Black Details

Use a thin brush and black paint to draw the nose shape on the tip of the child's nose.

Add black whiskers extending from the white cheeks.

Draw small black lines above the eyes to add expressive details.

Step 5: Add Details on Forehead and Cheeks

Use a thin brush to add small white lines on the forehead and cheeks, creating a fur effect.

Step 6: Finishing Touches

Ensure all lines are clear and the colors are well filled in. Show the child the final design in a mirror.

Step 7: Clean Up

Wash brushes and sponges with warm, soapy water. Test paints on a small skin area before painting.

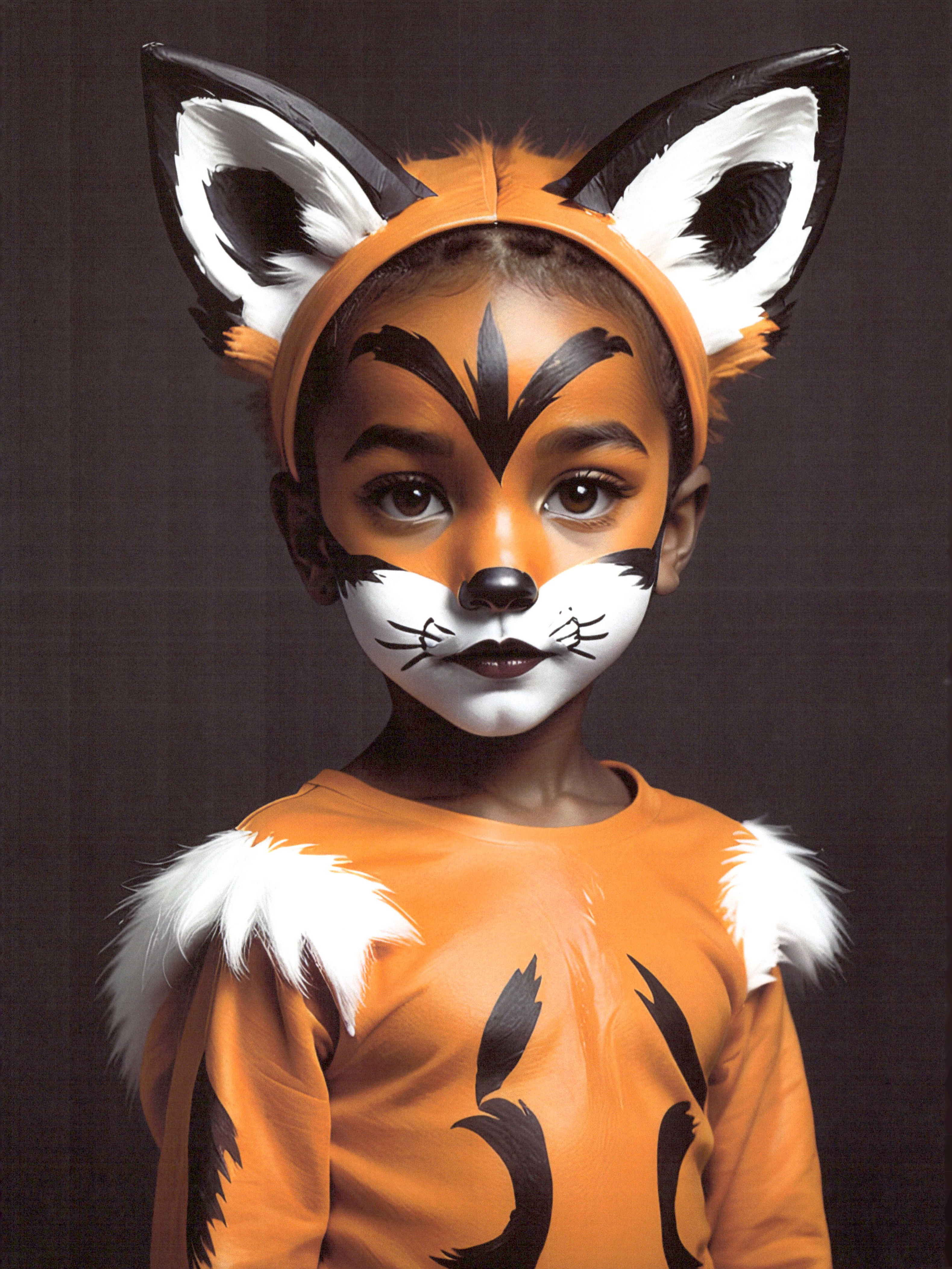

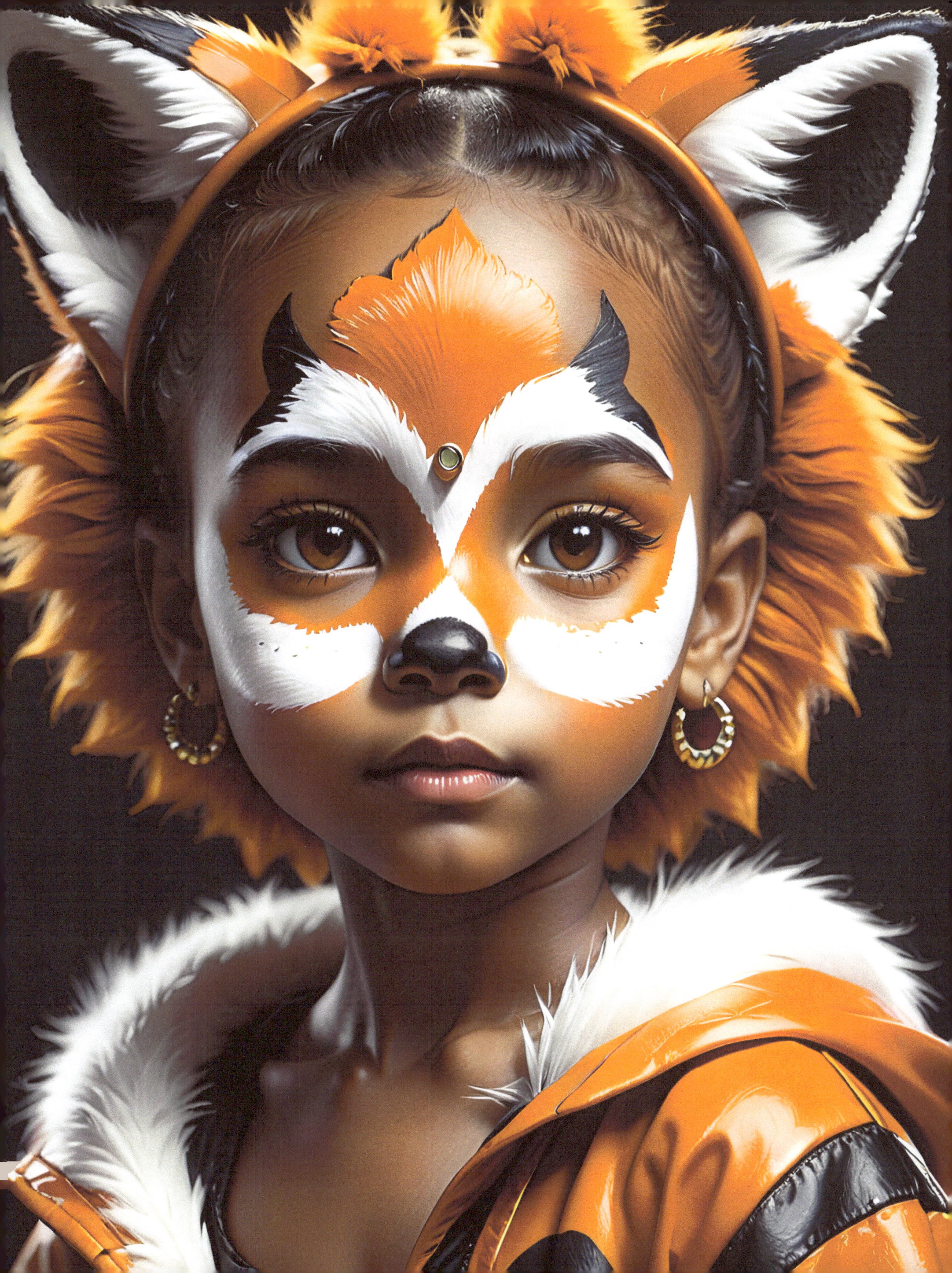

Face Painting Instructions: Frog Theme – Step by Step

Tools and Materials:

Face paints: green, white, black

Brushes: thin and medium

Sponge

Bowl of water

Tissues and paper towels

Mirror

Step 1: Prepare the Skin

Wash and dry the child's face.

Step 2: Apply the Green Base

Use a sponge to apply green paint over the entire face, creating a uniform base. Let it dry.

Step 3: Add Darker Green Accents

Use a medium brush to add darker green accents on the forehead, cheeks, and around the eyes. Create shapes resembling spots and patches characteristic of frogs.

Step 4: Draw White Accents

Use a thin brush and white paint to draw white dots and lines around the dark green patches. Add a few white dots on the cheeks to give the design an extra effect.

Draw larger white dots on the forehead to create the illusion of frog skin.

Step 5: Add Black Details

Use a thin brush and black paint to add black outlines around the white dots and patches. This will help to highlight the pattern and give it depth.

Add small black dots on the nose and around the eyes for extra detail.

Step 6: Add Details on Cheeks and Nose

Use a thin brush to add additional green, white, and black accents on the cheeks and nose, creating a more realistic frog look.

Step 7: Finishing Touches

Ensure all lines are clear and the colors are well filled in. Show the child the final design in a mirror.

Step 8: Clean Up

Wash brushes and sponges with warm, soapy water. Test paints on a small skin area before painting.

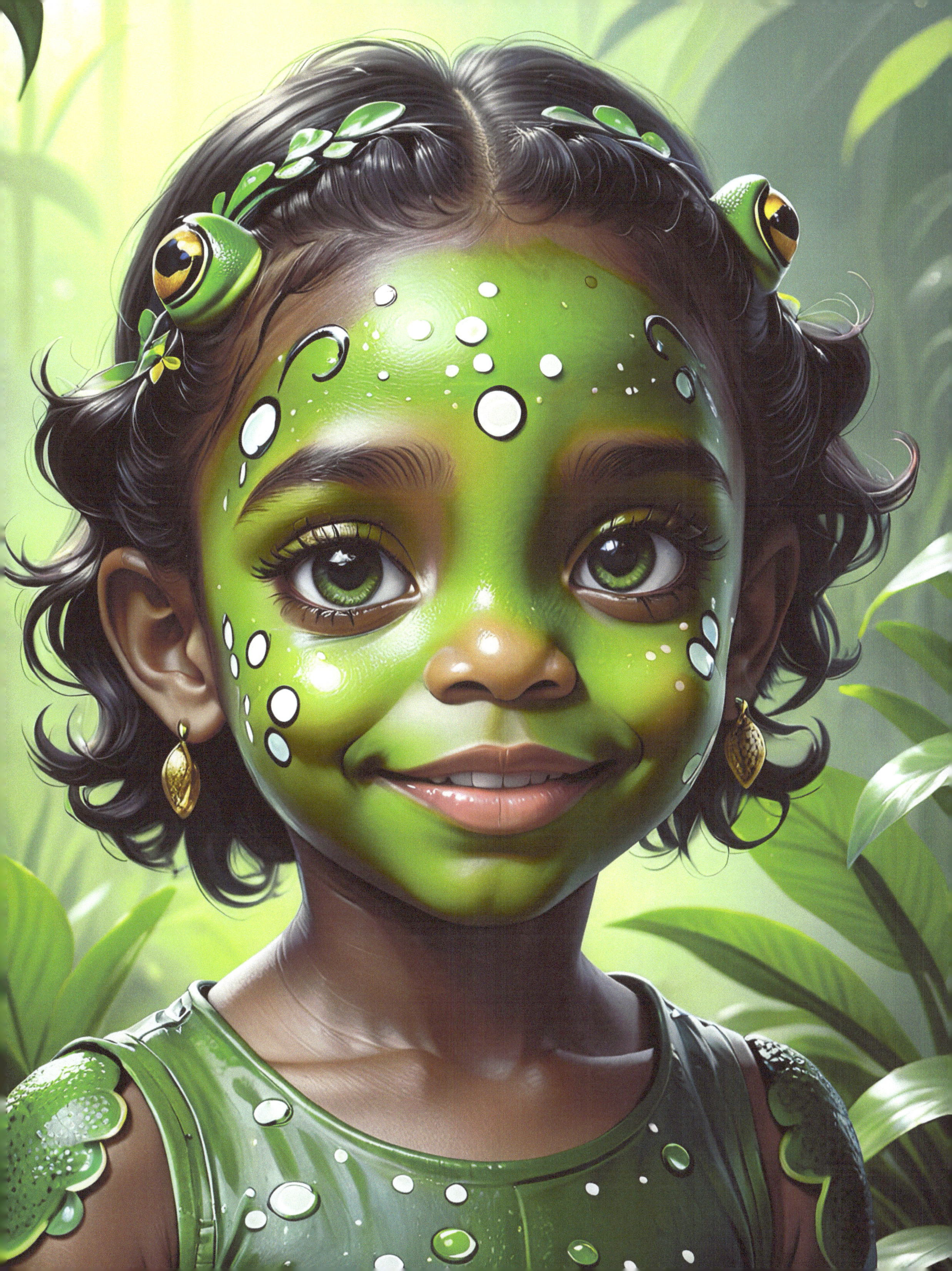

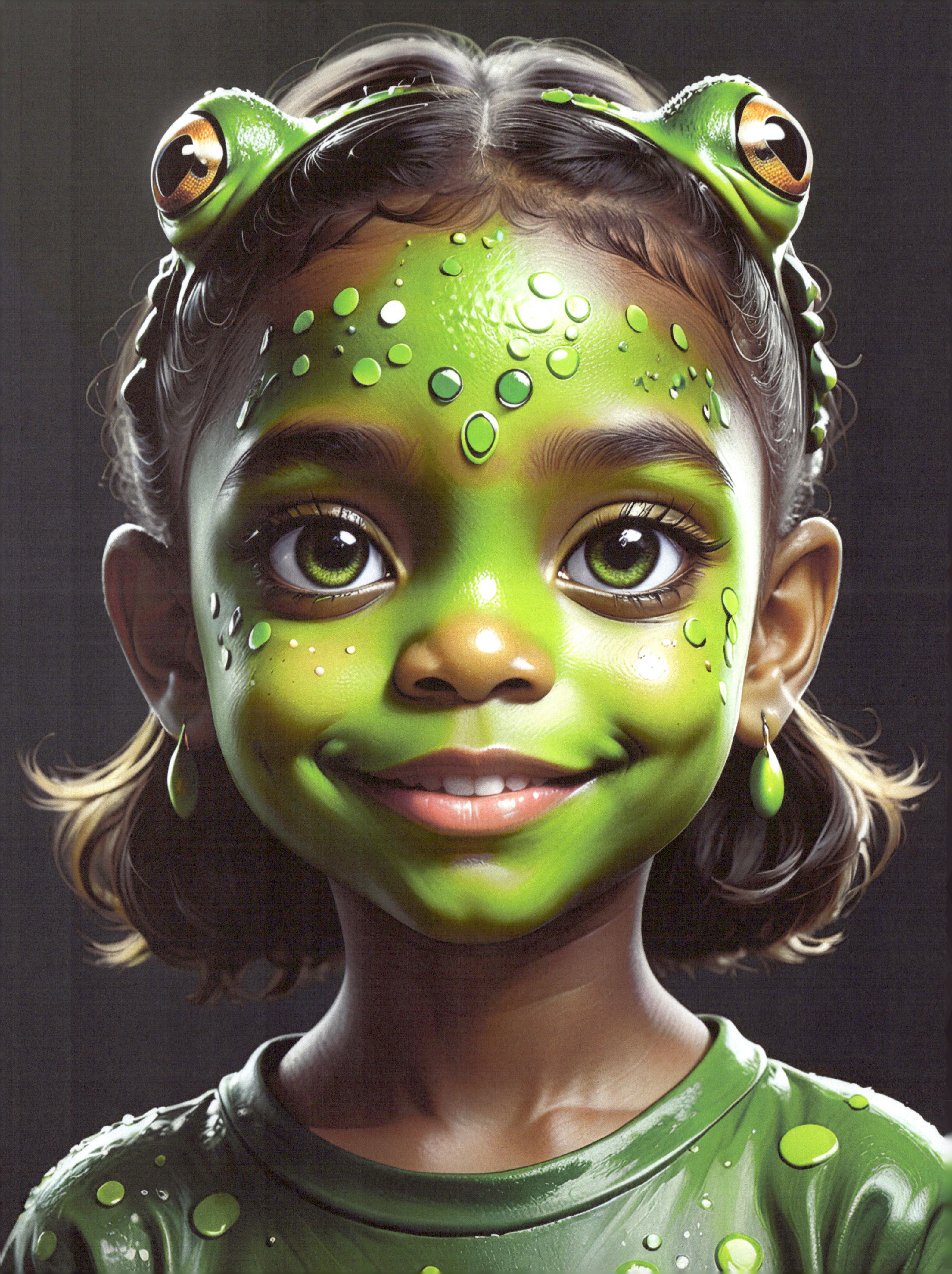

Thank You for Your Purchase

Dear Customer,

Thank you for purchasing our children's face painting book! We hope you find plenty of inspiration and joy while painting your child's face for various events and parties.

Your feedback is extremely important to us. If you enjoy the book or have any suggestions about its content, please share your thoughts with us. Your input helps us improve our products and better meet the expectations of our customers.

You can leave a review on the site where you made your purchase.

Once again, thank you for choosing our book. We wish you lots of fun with face painting!

Best regards,

The Life Style Daily Team